to Beverly M Gaines Mr. -

choices

bring ~~~~ ~~ llment!

nt,

Mike Magee m

Other books by Mike Magee, MD

Positive Doctors in America
Spencer Books, NY 1999

The Best Medicine
St. Martins Press, NY 1999

Positive Leadership
Spencer Books, NY 2000

The New Face of Aging
Spencer Books, NY 2001

**Order Information 1-800-774-3313,
or www.positiveprofiles.com**

The

Book

of

Choices

A Treasury of Insights for Personal and Professional Growth

Mike Magee, MD

Library of Congress Cataloging-in-Publication Data
Magee, Mike
The Book of Choice/Mike Magee, MD
328p. 17 x 12 cm.

1. Magee, Mike 2. Leadership 3. Interper-
sonal Relations
I. Title

BF 637.L4   2002   158.4
ISBN 1-889793-10-8
Manufactured in Canada
First Edition

To Anabella, her mother Susanna, her father Michael, her aunt Meredith, her uncles Mitchell and Marc, and her grandmothers Trish and Barbara

CONTENTS

Foreword   *x*

Choices

Foreward

As I approached the threshold of 50 years, then passed it, I became acutely aware of three things. First, that the course that my family and I had taken was the result of thousands of small and large decisions that we had made, day in and day out, over the years, rather than the product of luck or chance. Using the best information available at the time, and considering the competing interests of different members of our family, we made choices, and the choices as they accumulated defined our lives.

The second revelation was that the challenges we confronted as individuals and as a family, the decisions we faced and judgments we made, were not unique. The names, faces, locations and time in history were unique, but the challenges, tradeoffs and mysteries were much the same as those the human family has always faced. Understanding that, and looking back, taking stock, I decided to seek out what accumulated wisdom I could find in the form of quotes, preserved I believe because they captured some essence of living and resonated as useful and truthful.

The third insight was to involve others who I trusted and who were younger and perhaps less tainted than I in the selection process of the quotes. For this I turned primarily to my daughter Meredith, who spent the summer between her junior and senior year of college wading through some 20,000 quotations with the simple instruction from me to "circle those worth remembering." At the very least, I thought this would be a formative exercise for her and provide me interesting insight into our youngest child as she approached her 21st birthday.

The circled quotes were relatively few and far between. Each was insightful. Others were added by myself, my wife and our other children. I then spent several months reading the collected quotes carefully, reflecting on them, and drawing from them the principles and choices that were imbedded. Out of that exercise evolved 77 life choices which served as general categories for the 780 quotes that ultimately survived aggressive editing. Faced now with 77 groupings each housing between five and twenty quotes, I took each collection individually and created a simple passage that might aid the reader in reflecting on "the choice" at hand (e.g. to serve self or others, to be courageous or fearful, to be spiritual or material).

My words are accompanied by the quotations from which they were derived so that you may benefit from both the source and the output. Brief biographies on my source experts appear in the appendix section so that you might "consider the source". The final work then is a unified composite, a personal journey that attempts to capture points of guidance and direction from the finest minds throughout the centuries. My goals are simple, to support personal reflection and growth, and to have a positive impact on the choices you make which will define your life and the lives of the many others you will touch.

I quote others in order to better express my own self.

—Montaigne

Choice / Chance

Who to blame and who to credit for our successes and our failures? What is the face of fate; is it friendly or is it cruel? That there are obstacles, limits, barriers for each of us along the way is undeniable. They take many forms. Too many resources can as easily short-circuit growth as can too little. But destiny is determined by the choices, by what we make of our circumstances. There are parts of our lives that clearly escape any personal control, to whom we were born to name but one. But they are balanced more than equally by choices of free will. We choose, we work, we acquire both the good and the bad, we take these choices and analyze the results in the hope that the knowledge gained will result in better choices the next time around. This is how we learn to master chance. Our minds become prepared by choosing and embracing new paths. And if wrong, there's another fork up a little way around the curve and out of sight making it impossible to predict or plan. Make your choices, live with them, learn from them.

Whatever limits us we call Fate.
- Ralph Waldo Emerson

Destiny is not a matter of chance, it is a matter of choice; it is not a thing to be waited for, but a thing to be achieved.
- William Jennings Bryan

Chance makes our parents, but choice makes our friends.
- Jacques Delille

Work and acquire, and thou hast chained the wheel of Chance.
- Ralph Waldo Emerson

Chance favors the prepared mind.
- Louis Pasteur

Two roads diverged in a wood and I –
I took the one less traveled by,
And that has made all the difference.
- Robert Frost

How to make God laugh.
Tell him your future plans.
- Woody Allen

Happy / Unhappy

The truth be told, life is a challenge. Yet on its
surface ripples unpredictable currents of happiness intermixed with hopes and dreams.
These small visions of the future at first may be
simply self-entertaining. But then there comes
the spark, the realization that a dream – with
work, with help—could actually happen.
Worry and fear, if given into, can prevent the
transition. If not, the happiness can be found
in doses large enough to sustain the dream and
move a person toward goodness. An enemy of
the good is the better – better than now, better
than the other person. For this is a fundamental lack of gratitude for blessings at hand.
Happiness must be ridden, used, appreciated
as a form of transport, without the driving
obsession for what's next, always what's next.
In its simplicity, some happiness is attainable
by nearly everyone, even those whose burden
is unimaginable. Out of the quiet, it emerges
from within, and from without is reinforced by
good fortune from time to time. Happiness is
nurtured by action, and degraded by stasis,
by being stuck, powerless and risk averse.
Happiness can make you soar, but it can not

make you strong. The strength must lie in another vein, drawn upon to sustain you in those moments when happiness has vanished, drawn upon to sustain you until happiness returns.

Happiness is the light on the water. The water is cold and dark and deep.
-       William Maxwell

Knowledge of what is possible is the beginning of happiness.
-       George Santayana

There is only one way to happiness and that is to cease worrying about things which are beyond the power of our will.
-       Epictetus

The good life, as I conceive it, is a happy life. I do not mean that if you are good you will be happy – I mean that if you are happy you will be good.
-       Bertrand Russell

If we only wanted to be happy it would be easy; but we want to be happier than other people, which is always difficult, since we think them happier than they are.
-       Charles de Montesquieu

Remember that happiness is a way of travel – not a destination.
-       Roy M. Goodman

If you don't enjoy getting up and working and finishing your work and sitting down to a meal with family or friends, then the chances are you're not going to be happy. If someone bases his happiness or unhappiness on major events like a great new job, huge amounts of money, a flawlessly happy marriage or a trip to Paris,

20

that person isn't going to be happy much of the time. If, on the other hand, happiness depends on a good breakfast, flowers in the yard, a drink or a nap, then we are more likely to live with quite a bit of happiness.

- Andy Rooney

True happiness is of a retired nature and an enemy to pomp and noise; it arises, in the first place, from the enjoyment of one's self; and, in the next, from the friendship and conversation of a few selected companions.

- Joseph Addison

The amount of satisfaction you get from life depends largely on your own ingenuity, self-sufficiency, and resourcefulness. People who wait around for life to supply their satisfaction usually find boredom instead.

- Dr. William Menninger

It's pretty hard to tell what does bring happiness; poverty and wealth have both failed.

- Kin Hubbard

Happiness makes up in height for what it lacks in strength.

- Robert Frost

Love / Hate

What do two imperfect souls have to offer each other beyond a touch, a smile, a willingness to defend? Each smile has a future that's built in, made certain by a confidence in the "better or worse", "richer or poorer", "in sickness and in health", or not. How tender is that early touch, how daring their belief that it will last. And when it does, only later do the children learn how precious the gift of loyalty their parents gave. Or if it goes the other way, how deep the wounds and their hostility. And if they had the chance to redo how many would decide to just give love and not attempt to carry each and every day, to win each and every self created skirmish. Is it possible to disengage, to decide that the burden of hate, even momentary, is too great? Is it possible to believe that little losses given willingly can create a hearty truth that is expressed as confidence and trust and love, and that this can be achieved only when two agree to play. Lovers understand that loving is not the same as winning, but more about creating.

Love consists in this, that two solitudes protect and touch and greet each other.
-    Rainer Maria Rilke

They gave each other a smile with a future in it.
-    Ring Lardner

The bravest things are the tenderest. The loving are the daring.
-    Henry Wadsworth Longfellow

The most important thing a father can do for his children is to love their mother.
-    Theodore Hesburgh

If we could read the secret history of our enemies, we should find in each man's life, sorrow and suffering enough to disarm all hostility.
-    Henry Wadsworth Longfellow

Do not inflict your will. Just give love. The soul will take that love and put it where it can best be used.
-    Emmanuel

Don't hate, it's too big a burden to bear.
-    Martin Luther King, Sr.

Between whom there is a hearty truth, there is love.
-    Henry David Thoreau

Love, and do what you like.
-    St. Augustine

Spiritual / Material

There is a natural communication that goes on between the material and the spiritual worlds. Humans struggle for a means of expression. Nature responds, at moments of openness, to each individual, and to each in its own way. To some, the connection to the spirit is direct, to others through individuals who possess some of the characteristics sought. For all, there is a delicate but discordant balance struck between what we know to be true on any given day, and what we believe, or trust, or hope to be true for an eternity. If there is tension, it is in deciding which world will guide when path ways crisis and cross. There are times when the spirit has the upper hand, as there are times when ignoring the facts places all at risk. Learning when and how to rely on one, the other, or both is a slow and difficult process. So it is best to begin each day anew. For in daily life, each is called to steer a course, to make decisions for better or worse, and live with and learn from the results. This requires enterprise and bravery. And in moments of self doubt and hesitation, there is the spirit to lean on, knowing that, in the end, each has done her best and will be rewarded for the effort.

24

Art is man's nature; nature is God's art.
- P. J. Bailey

God enters by a private door into every individual.
- Ralph Waldo Emerson

A great man stands on God. A small man stands on a greater man.
- Ralph Waldo Emerson

Science without religion is lame, religion without science is blind.
- Albert Einstein

The means by which we live have outdistanced the ends for which we live. Our scientific power has outrun our spiritual power. We have guided missiles and misguided men.
- Martin Luther King, Jr.

To have a curable illness and to leave it untreated except for prayer is like sticking your hand in a fire and asking God to remove the flame.
- Sandra L. Douglas

The Lord's Prayer may be committed to memory quickly, but it is slowly learnt by heart.
- Frederick Denison Maurice

Don't wait for the Last Judgment. It takes place every day.
- Albert Camus

The Ancient Mariner said to Neptune during a great storm, 'O God, you will save me if you wish, but I am going to go on holding my tiller straight.'
- Michel de Montaigne

What recommends commerce to me is its enterprise and bravery. It does not clasp its hands and pray to Jupiter.
- Henry David Thoreau

The spirit indeed is willing, but the flesh is weak.
- Matthew 26:41

If there is another world, he lives in bliss
If there is none, he made the best of this.
- Robert Burns

Engaged / Indifferent

Once committed, fortune follows. Ignorance is
a convenient excuse for disengagement. To not
care is to lack magic and power. To wait for
others to intervene is simply to admit one's
powerlessness, to admit that one is without life
– lifeless. It is more about the living and less
about the wondering what might have been.
The world is a dangerous place. So what?
Now what? Never be neutral. Stand for something. Those who "couldn't care less" force
each of us to care more. Worse than evil –
indifference to evil. Emerge, embrace, embody
a belief and you will cease to be afraid. It is
okay to be wrong, as long as you think and feel
each day. Be not a cold and timid soul. Be
biased toward pursuit.

There is one elementary truth, the ignorance of which kills countless ideas and splendid plans: the moment one definitely commits oneself, then Providence moves too. All sorts of things occur to help one that never otherwise would have occurred...
Whatever you can do,
Or dream you can do,
Begin it.
Boldness has genius, power and magic in it.
Begin it now.
- Goethe

If there is a sin against life, it consists perhaps not so much in despairing of life as in hoping for another, and in eluding the implacable grandeur of this life.
- Albert Camus

Live all you can; it's a mistake not to. It doesn't so much matter what you do in particular, so long as you have your life. If you haven't had that, what *have* you had?
- Henry James

Life is to be lived. If you have to support yourself, you had bloody well better find some way that is going to be interesting. And you don't do that by sitting around wondering about yourself.
- Katharine Hepburn

The world is a dangerous place to live – not because of the people who are evil but because of the people who don't do anything about it.
- Albert Einstein

The hottest places in hell are reserved for those who, in time of great moral crisis, maintain their neutrality.
-   Dante

The true opposite of love is not hate but indifference. Hate, bad as it is, at least treats the neighbor as a thou, whereas indifference turns the neighbor into an it, a thing. This is why we may say that there is actually one thing worse than evil itself and that is indifference to evil. In human relations the nadir of morality, the lowest point as far as Christian ethics is concerned, is manifest in the phrase, 'I couldn't care less.'
-   Joseph Fletcher

Become so wrapped up in something that you forget to be afraid.
-   Lady Bird Johnson

I wish to say what I think and feel today, with the proviso that tomorrow perhaps I shall contradict it all.
-   Ralph Waldo Emerson

It is not the critic who counts, not the man who points out the strong man stumbled, or where the doer of the deeds could have done better. The credit belongs to the man who is actually in the arena; whose face is marred by the dust and sweat and blood; who strives valiantly; who errs and comes short again and again; who knows the great enthusiasms, the great devotions and spends himself in a worthy course; who at the best, knows in the end the triumph of high achievement, and who, at worst, if he fails, at least fails while daring greatly; so that his place shall never be with those cold and timid souls who know neither victory or defeat.

                    -    Teddy Roosevelt

The crowning blessing of life- to be born with a bias to some pursuit.

                    -    S. G. Tallentyre

Patient / Impatient

Patience is not stasis but pace. Patience is not retreat but rather a form of preparation. Humans are most impatient with themselves, expecting growth without leaving time for maturity, expecting perfection from imperfect creatures, expecting pleasure without pain. Patience is realistic but hopeful. Patience is delay, not denial, a determined vision that holds fast. Patience is sensitive to time. For success is rarely, almost never, probably never, instantaneous. It is not the nature of things to ripen from the start. The environment must have its say. First blossom, then the fruit to age in color, texture and good taste. To go through all that is to be worthy of selection. To shorten the process in a burst of self-will may get a person picked but then discarded with first bite, not ripe enough, not yet.

Have patience with all things, but chiefly have patience with yourself. Do not lose courage in considering your own imperfections, but instantly set about remedying them – every day begin the task anew.

- St. Francis de Sales

Never think that God's delays are God's denials. Hold on, hold fast; hold out. Patience is genius.

- Comte de Buffon

They also serve who only stand and wait.

- John Milton

Actually, I'm an overnight success. But it took twenty years.

- Monty Hall

Nothing great is created suddenly, any more than a bunch of grapes or a fig. If you tell me that you desire a fig, I answer you that there must be time. Let it first blossom, then bear fruit, then ripen.

- Epictetus

Kind / Mean

Of all the gifts we have to offer each other, kindness is of greatest value to the most people. Human kindness is instinctive but must be modeled to take hold. As the individual moves toward independence, kindness will compete with other instincts like exclusion, fear, and self-interest. Kindness must be bred in, well-established, incapable of detachment. It must also be exercised by societal expectations that reinforce "better to be kind than mean". Kindness should not be held hostage to pretenders who smile only for a purpose, who reach out only to pull back in. Kindness is its own reward. Kindness works against the opposite which seeks to diminish, to belittle, to isolate. Unkindness ultimately is most unkind to those who are its source. One should not wait to be kind. There is no one perfect time. Every time is a perfect time.

One kind word can warm three winter months.
-       Japanese saying

If you would civilize a man, begin with his grandmother.
-       Victor Hugo

Good breeding, a union of kindness and independence.
-       Ralph Waldo Emerson

Civilization is just a slow process of learning to be kind.
-       Charles L. Lucas

The teeth are smiling, but is the heart?
-       Congo proverb

It takes your enemy and your friend, working together
to hurt you to the heart; the one to slander you and the
other to get the news to you.
-       Mark Twain

I expect to pass through this world but once. Any good
therefore that I can do, or any kindness that I can show
to my fellow-creature, let me do it now. Let me not defer
or neglect it, for I shall not pass this way again.
-       Stephen Grellet

Hope / Despair

Hope resides in the future, in the possibility, in the blessings, lessons, redemption not yet visible. Whether the light comes from within or without is unclear. But this we know, it can only be extinguished as a voluntary act. This is not to say that people have no reason to despair. There are practically no limits to the reasons, at one time or another, in every life. The fortunate and the unfortunate suffer. And yet hope survives in part on the knowledge that pain, insecurity and deeply embedded doubt carry with them sparkling moments of insight and redemption. It is easier to hope in company, with others showing the way. But never easy. Still, when given the choice, even were the destination the same, would you rather go in hope or in despair? So cry out if you will, for at least you're crying out (to something) and not crying in (to nothing). And do we not often find a way? If we look around inside and out, at small problems and large, isn't life a mixture of suffering and overcoming it? It is not a certain world. But if the dice are to be rolled, who's to say you won't come up a winner soon. You can't see around the corner, nor find the secret gate, without stepping around the corner, reaching out. Our strength, our light lies in our roots, deep inside. The desire to survive, to resist, to love, to protect, to care and be cared for. Fear not!

Hope springs eternal in the human breast;
Man never is, but always *to be* blest.
>   -   Alexander Pope

Even in the deepest sinking there is the hidden purpose of an ultimate rising. Thus it is for all men, from none is the source of light withheld unless he himself withdraws from it. Therefore the most important thing is not to despair.
>   -   Hasidic Saying

When it is dark enough, you can see the stars.
>   -   Charles A. Beard

Hope is like a road in the country; there was never a road, but when many people walk on it, the road comes into existence.
>   -   Lin Yutang

It has never been, and never will be, easy work! But the road that is built in hope is more pleasant to the traveler than the road built in despair, even though they lead to the same destination.
>   -   Marion Zimmer Bradley

Even the cry from the depths is an affirmation: why cry if there is no hint or hope of hearing?
>   -   Martin Marty

Although the world is full of suffering, it is full also of the overcoming of it.
>   -   Helen Keller

In the face of uncertainty, there is nothing wrong with hope.

> \-   Bernie S. Siegel, M.D.

Still round the corner there may wait,
A new road, or a secret gate.

> \-   J. R. R. Tolkein

Deep in their roots,
All flowers keep the light.

> \-   Theodore Roethke

When fear is excessive it can make many a man despair.

> \-   Saint Thomas Aquinas

Useful / Useless

There are needs and there are people who fill these needs. The needs are as vast and diverse as are the skills that humans possess to respond. How needs and skills match up is part organization and part personal motivation. But one thing is certain, if you wish to be useful you can. Each of us possesses an ability that is needed by someone somewhere. To be useful adds value on both sides of the equation. It clearly benefits the individual in receipt but also is formative for the offerer, forming her as a human being. To possess skills and not share them is self-destructive. Holding back holds you back. Equally, the inability to utilize one's skills for the productive benefit of others because individuals are unwilling to provide the opportunity is a frustration that rapidly leads to resentment and self-loathing. It is as important to be needed as it is important to be useful. Everyone's work matters. Everyone's job is worth doing well. Each person's effort is as unique as each vision of the world, each touch, each thought, each deed. Each individual matters – from the first day of life to the last.

Find a need and fill it.
- Ruth Stafford Peale

If heaven made him, earth can find some use for him.
- Chinese proverb

Not only must we be good, but we must also be good for something.
- Henry David Thoreau

There's no labor a man can do that's undignified, if he does it right.
- Bill Cosby

If a man is called to be a street sweeper, he should sweep streets even as Michelangelo painted, or Beethoven composed music, or Shakespeare wrote poetry. He should sweep streets so well that all the hosts of heaven and earth will pause to say, here lived a great street sweeper who did his job well.
- Martin Luther King, Jr.

I really believe there are things nobody would see if I didn't photograph them.
- Diane Arbus

On the day of his death, in his eightieth year, Elliot, 'the Apostle of the Indians,' was found teaching an Indian child at his bedside. 'Why not to rest from your labors now?' asked a friend. 'Because,' replied the venerable man, 'I have prayed God to render me useful in my sphere, and he has heard my prayers; for now that I can no longer preach, he leaves me strength enough to teach this poor child the alphabet.'
- S. Chaplin

Simple / Complex

Less, not more. So that you can focus without
distraction, appreciating loveliness in its most
natural and naturally appearing state, without
a price attached or a quid pro quo. Simple
truths emerge from the greatest spirits, and
simple spirits voice the greatest truths. Simple
involvement to the point of oneness with one's
work can, in the absence of purpose, direction,
aim or meaning still bring happiness. That is
the mystery, the power of alignment. Complexity is never of value where simplicity will
suffice. Leave alone as much as you can, as
much as you will – in word, in deed, in material. Need creates greater need, and less of
everything else. With simple prayers, the
likelihood of a good response is heightened
creating a state of happiness in those who have
little visible reason to rejoice beyond the fact
that they are happy still.

Simplicity, simplicity, simplicity. I say, let your affairs be as two or three, and not a hundred or a thousand; instead of a million count half a dozen, and keep your accounts on your thumbnail.

-   Henry David Thoreau

And all the loveliest things there be
Come simply, so it seems to me.

-   Edna St. Vincent Millay

That man is richest whose pleasures are the cheapest.

-   Henry David Thoreau

The greatest truths are the simplest, and so are the greatest men.

-   J. C. and A.W. Hare

My life has no purpose, no direction, no aim, no meaning, and yet I'm happy. I can't figure it out. What am I doing right?

-   Charles M. Schulz

Some of the papers presented at today's medical meeting tell us what we already know, but in a much more complicated manner.

-   Alphonse Raymond Dochez

The fewer the words, the better the prayer.

-   Martin Luther

The happiest people seem to be those who have no particular cause for being happy except that they are so.

-   William Ralph Inge

Observe / Ignore

The basis of most learning, most decisions, and most growth is observation. The brightest stars see beyond the obvious to the signals that precede the obvious. They observe with equal attention what works and what does not work. They are careful to remember failures for their special power to instruct. Mistakes after all are acceptable. Repetition is not. To observe is an active state, the ability to see beneath the surface calm and detect the turbulence below. The small observation neglected translates into matters of greater consequence. It's the little things, the little things. The difference between good and great is attention to detail.

Certain signs precede certain events.

> \- Cicero

Results! Why, man, I have gotten a lot of results. I know several thousand things that won't work.

> \- Thomas A. Edison

In every work of genius we recognize our own rejected thoughts; they come back to us with a certain alienated majesty.

> \- Ralph Waldo Emerson

There is nothing wrong with making mistakes. Just don't respond with encores.

> \- Anon.

You can observe a lot just by watching.

> \- Yogi Berra

Don't think there are no crocodiles because the water is calm.

> \- Malayan proverb

A little neglect may breed great mischief... For want of a nail, the shoe was lost; for want of a shoe, the horse was lost; for want of a horse, the battle was lost; for want of the battle, the war was lost.

> \- Benjamin Franklin

Feel / Think

In a task-driven society it is not surprising that thinking is held in such high and serious regard. It after all is the engine producing the raw materials of the mind, some of which, a few of which prove to be of lasting value. But to feel is to be alive, and that is quite a different thing. One advances with experience, the other is most profound it seems in the inexperienced. One is focused on what things are, the other on what might be. One is sustained by facts and figures, the other swallows whole an image or sound or smell and is surprised. One has muscle, the other personality. One has words, the other color. One describes around the edges, the other penetrates deep within, taking words and transforming them into poetry.

One looks back with appreciation on the brilliant teachers, but with gratitude to those who touched our human feelings. The curriculum is so much necessary raw material, but warmth is a vital element for the growing plant and for the soul of the child.

- Carl Jung

Experience is in the fingers and the head. The heart is inexperienced.

- Henry David Thoreau

Man is the only animal that laughs and weeps; for he is the only animal that is struck by the difference between what things are and what they might have been.

- William Hazlitt

The sky is the daily bread of the eyes.

- Ralph Waldo Emerson

We should take care not to make intellect out god; it has, of course, powerful muscles, but no personality.

- Albert Einstein

If you could say it in words there would be no reason to paint.

- Edward Hopper

For words, like Nature, half reveal
And half conceal the Soul within.

- Alfred, Lord Tennyson

Painting is silent poetry, and poetry is painting with the gift of speech.

- Simonides

Content / Driven

Fame is clearly a double edged sword. Ambition drives many to the edge of the cliff, some over. And looking down, for most of us, there is an inner force, drawing us back, within ourselves, to reflect and search again for peace. Moments of calm are spiritual, transcendent, contrasting with the reckless pursuit of success which overtakes the driven and drives them into the ground, buried and untouched by the simple breezes – sensation, touch, expression. Feeling cheated, that is the problem; that you deserve better, and for less effort. All of this done to seize the very things that would on surface appear to offer comfort and insulation but in fact draw you farther from the goals – simplicity, self-sufficiency, and inner strength. To be content and to think about being content are not the same thing, no more than planning to be can ever match being in the moment itself. Contentment is by definition not thought out. It is offered only to those who are ready to receive. It is a subtly graded sensation, heightened by its moderation rather than its intensity, causing one to marvel that a moment so simple and ordinary could be so fine. Those moments are recognizable by the joy and peace built in, by freedom from the pressing need to fix or mend a problem, an injury or a hurt. These are the moments of acceptance, of living, of observation, of freedom from worry, valued for the infrequency of their appearance. And these gifts, when they appear, just as quickly disappear if not recognized immediately for what they are. For here is the deceit – they are so normal in their trappings that they appear to be devoid of value until the last moment. In the end, it comes to most of us that suspending the need to save the world from time to time may be required to savor it.

All the fame I look for in life is to have lived it quietly.
-     Montaigne

The trouble with the rat race is that even if you win,
you're still a rat.
-     Lily Tomlin

If all our misfortunes were laid in one common heap,
whence everyone must take an equal portion, most
people would be content to take their own and depart.
-     Socrates

The lust for comfort, that stealthy thing that enters the
house as a guest and then becomes a host, and then a
master.
-     Kahlil Gibran

Thinking about interior peace destroys interior peace.
The patient who constantly feels his pulse is not getting
any better.
-     Hubert van Zeller

Better a little fire to warm us than a great one to burn us.
-     Thomas Fuller

Life is about enjoying yourself and having a good time.
-     Cher

O God, give us serenity to accept what cannot be
changed, courage to change what should be changed;
and wisdom to distinguish one from the other.
-     Reinhold Niebuhr

I don't like money actually, but it quiets my nerves.
-    Joe Louis

Strange how few
After all's said and done, the things that are
Of moment.
-    Edna St Vincent Millay

The days come and go like muffled and veiled figures
sent from a distant friendly party, but they say nothing,
and if we do not use the gifts they bring, they carry them
as silently away.
-    Ralph Waldo Emerson

Normal day, let me be aware of the treasure you are. Let
me learn from you, love you, bless you before you
depart. Let me not pass you by in quest of some perfect
tomorrow. Let me hold you while I may, for it may not
always be so. One day I shall dig my nails into the
earth, or bury my face in the pillow, or stretch myself
taut, or raise my hands to the sky and want, more than
all the world, your return.
-    Mary Jean Iron

If the world were merely seductive, that would be easy.
If it were merely challenging, that would be no problem.
But I rise in the morning torn between a desire to
improve (or save) the world and a desire to enjoy (or
savor) the world. This makes it hard to plan the day.
-    E. B. White

Accept / Reject

We are a wounded people, wounded from the start, wounded at the last. Not bad, not deserving of ill fortune, but imperfect, each and every one. The wounds are unique, as different one from another as the differences of one individual from the next. But wounded still. The wise society is prepared to respond, the enlightened society is positioned to invite and accept. That the wounded will always need embraces and will reach upward in response to greet their finer selves provides a purpose for government and her people. Inquire about those with the most pressing needs, seek them out. Out of their failures addressed come all of our successes. Out of the small battles come large victories. It is a world of helpers or hurters. To be the former, be prepared to criticize and to accept criticism often undeserved. Helping and happiness don't always coexist. You can catch hell for helping. What helping will do is always fill a space, a void in your life or in another's or both, and draw the dawn nearer for all.

With malice toward none, with charity for all, with firmness in the right as God gives us to see the right, let us strive on to finish the work we are in, to bind up the nations wounds.

- Abraham Lincoln,
  Second Inaugural Address

Send these, the homeless, tempest toss'd, to me. I lift my lamp beside the golden door

- Emma Lazarus
  (Inscription on the
  Statue of Liberty)

Pick battles big enough to matter, small enough to win.

- Jonathan Kozol

The difference between good and bad, better and worse, is simply helping or hurting.

- Ralph Waldo Emerson

He has a right to criticize who has a heart to help.

- Abraham Lincoln

Everything I did in my life that was worthwhile I caught hell for.

- Earl Warren, Chief Justice
  U.S. Supreme Court

There remain times when one can only endure. One lives on, one doesn't die, and the only thing that one can do, is to fill one's mind and time as far as possible with the concerns of other people. It doesn't bring immediate peace, but it brings the dawn nearer.

- Arthur Christopher Benson

Include / Exclude

Exclusion creates a special brand of loneliness made worse again by distrust or lack of confidence. The world has witnessed many forms of exclusion, each justified with its own convoluted rationale, but none that has stood the test of time, or reason, or good sense. Excluding sets in motion changes that eventually overtake the excluder, for he is an instrument of the status quo. Nations within nations are unhealthy, pitting the we against the they, creating neighborhoods without brotherhood. To be different has its strengths, to be unafraid of striking out anew, to advance rather than withdraw. For we know a country's future mission is reflected in the eyes and point of view of its minority citizens, as is its past reinforced by the majority. Excluded people are tougher than the rest, strengthened by the constant hammering, separated and rising to the top like cream on milk. So why shake it, and make it all the same? Rather make it safe to be different. Inclusion celebrates all.

What loneliness is more lonely than distrust.
- George Eliot

The world is white no longer, and it will never be white again.
- James Baldwin

It is not healthy when a nation lives within a nation, as coloured Americans are living inside America. A nation cannot live confident of its tomorrow if its refugees are among its own citizens.
- Pearl Buck

The world has narrowed to a neighborhood before it has broadened to a brotherhood.
- Lyndon B. Johnson

It is always the minorities that hold the key of progress; it is always through those who are unafraid to be different that advance comes to human society.
- Raymond B. Fosdick

Shall we judge a country by the majority, or by the minority? By the minority, surely.
- Ralph Waldo Emerson

The nail that sticks out is hammered down.
- Japanese proverb

If we cannot now end our differences, at least we can help make the world safe for diversity.
- John F. Kennedy

Freedom / Bondage

The human race throughout all time has been subjected to many forms of bondage. Freedom has been the response, the willingness to take a chance understanding that ~~the worst is already today's reality.~~ With all else gone, the chains are broken. What do we fight for? To speak our mind and disapprove. To be unencumbered by brutality and restrictions to growth and self development. To be unpopular. To be responsible for ourselves. Achieving freedom and practicing freedom are not the same. Once gained, freedom must find expression in the vigilant pursuit of justice here at home. The pursuit of more can disappoint and lead directly to less, so fettered down may we become with things that do not matter, that we are no longer free to embrace and must be content to join at a point here or there, no longer free to think, just free to speak in tired words. "We hold these truths to be self-evident." Self-evident yes, but not secure without hard work and a decent respect.

Freedom is what you do with what's been done to you.
- Jean-Paul Sartre

Freedom is nothing else but a chance to be better, whereas enslavement is a certainty of the worst.
- Albert Camus

When you have robbed a man of everything, he is no longer in your power. He is free again.
- Aleksandr Solzhenitsyn

I disapprove of what you say, but I will defend to the death your right to say it.
- Voltaire

You have freedom when you're easy in your harness.
- Robert Frost

My definition of a free society is a society where it is safe to be unpopular.
- Adlai Stevenson

When the freedom they wished for most was the freedom of responsibility, then Athens ceased to be free and never was free again.
- Edith Hamilton

So free we seem, so fettered fast we are!
- Robert Browning

Lives based on having are less free than lives based on doing or on being.
- William James

True patriotism hates injustice in its own land more than anywhere else.

                          -     Clarence Darrow

When in the course of human events it becomes necessary for one people to dissolve the political bands which have connected them with another, and to assume among the powers of the earth the separate and equal station to which the laws of nature and of nature's God entitle them, a decent respect to the opinions of mankind requires that they should declare the causes which impel them to the separation. We hold these truths to be self evident; that all men are created equal; that they are endowed by their creator with certain unalienable rights; that among these are life, liberty, and the pursuit of happiness; that to secure these rights, governments are instituted among men, deriving their just powers from the consent of the governed; that whenever any form of government becomes destructive to these ends, it is the right of the people to alter or to abolish it, and to institute new government, laying its foundation on such principals, and organize its powers in such form, as to them shall seem most likely to effect their safety and happiness.

                          -     Thomas Jefferson, from the
                    Declaration of Independence (July 4, 1776)

What, to the American slave, is your 4th of July? I answer: a day that reveals to him, more than all the other days in the year, the gross injustice and cruelty to which he is the constant victim.

                          -     Frederick Douglass

Passionate / Cynical

Fervor flows with the first breath of life. In a perfect world, this stream of energy would be constant, relentless, unimpeded through all one's time. Yet life presents obstacles, both internal and external. Complacency finds its way through the door of comfort and luxury on the one hand or through the cracks of resignation and hopelessness on the other. The greatest civilizations have never lacked for passion, for seeking, for striving for a certain belief, an ideal that unleashed great thoughts and actions. People of reason rarely can compete with those whose interest is personal and complete. The juice flows with the first step and continues beyond the last, expecting nothing, fearing nothing. There are no detours. There is no turning back. The eye of passion is on the possible.

Happy the man who gains sagacity in youth, but thrice happy he who retains the fervor of youth in age.
-    Dogobert Runes

We act as though comfort and luxury were the chief requirements of life, when all that we need to make us really happy is something to be enthusiastic about.
-    Charles Kingsley

What our age lacks is not reflection but passion.
-    Søren Kierkegaard

I am seeking, I am striving, I am in it with all my heart.
-    Vincent van Gogh

The eloquent man is he who is no beautiful speaker, but who is inwardly and desperately drunk with a certain belief.
-    Ralph Waldo Emerson

Blessed is he who carries within himself a god and an ideal and who obeys it – an ideal of art, of science, or gospel virtues. Therein lie the springs of great thoughts and great actions.
-    Louis Pasteur

Would you persuade, speak of interest, not of reason.
-    Benjamin Franklin

As long as you can start, you are all right. The juice will come.
-    Ernest Hemingway

If thou workest at that which is before thee ... expecting nothing, fearing nothing, but satisfied with thy present activity according to Nature, and with heroic truth in every word and sound which thou utterest, thou wilt live happy. And there is no man who is able to prevent this.

- Marcus Aurelius

My face is set, my gait is fast, my goal is Heaven, my road is narrow, my way is rough, my companions are few, my guide is reliable, my mission is clear. I cannot be bought, compromised, detoured, lured away, turned back, diluted, or delayed. I will not flinch in the face of sacrifice, hesitate in the presence of adversity, negotiate ... at the table of the enemy, ponder at the pool of popularity, or meander in a maze of mediocrity. I won't give up, shut up, let up or slow up.

- Robert Moorehead

If I were to wish for anything, I should not wish for wealth and power, but for the passionate sense of the potential, for the eye which, ever young and ardent, sees the possible... what wine is so sparkling, so fragrant, so intoxicating, as possibility!

- Søren Kierkegaard

Perfection / Imperfection

None of us is perfect. We all have cracks, some more visible than others. But that does not mean that we shouldn't try to reach the stars, that we should intentionally sell short ourselves. We may be earthbound but we should be heaven bent. Commit to pursuing your highest aspirations. That's where the beauty lies. And even if you fall short, you will be better formed by the seeking process. People expect faults in human beings. It is our nature to make mistakes. Without this feature how would we support the desire to perfect ourselves, to improve ourselves and our lives. Tie in the fact that courage is centered here, both the courage to acknowledge imperfections and the courage to attempt the corrections. No one is perfect in all things. My worst may be assisted by your best and my best of value to your worst. Let's make a deal then. Let's both admit we're deeply flawed and commit together to a mutual correction.

There is a crack in everything God has made.
- Ralph Waldo Emerson

Aim at heaven and you get earth thrown in; aim at earth and you get neither.
- C.S. Lewis

Far away in the sunshine are my highest inspirations. I may not reach them, but I can look up and see the beauty, believe in them and try to follow where they lead.
- Louisa May Alcott

You're only human, you're supposed to make mistakes.
- Billy Joel

If a man wants to be of the greatest possible value to his fellow-creatures, let him begin the long, solitary task of perfecting himself.
- Robertson Davies

Do not lose courage in considering your own imperfections.
- Saint Francis de Sales

There is so much good in the worst of us and so much bad in the best of us, that it's rather hard to tell which of us ought to reform the rest of us.
- Sign in Springdale, CT

If the best man's faults were written on his forehead, it would make him pull his hat over his eyes.
- Gaelic Proverb

Change / Stasis

Progress requires change. A civil society attempts to accommodate this need through openness, transparency and inclusion. As there is change in society, so are there changes in individuals and relationships as well. Change can generate fear and anxiety, but also can ignite our inborn desire to explore, to flow and grow rather than remain the same. We are accustomed to a rhythm recognizing and accepting that no two days are alike in every way. Our days move quickly, flying by with little time to reflect or resist. That we are transitory, moving from one chore to the next, one person to the next, one location to the next is undeniable. Our placement is displacement, and our displacement is movement. But the movement keeps us fresh. Change for the better is self-improvement. Some prefer to stand still, to play it safe, to wait on the corner to be found, discovered, rescued. Some will be lucky. But the price this strategy extracts is a growing and eventually overpowering sense of powerlessness that over time may convert to bitterness. We were born to move, to move on, not so much to reach a destination but to find one.

The art of progress is to preserve order amid change, and to preserve change amid order.
- Alfred North Whitehead

All things flow, nothing abides.
- Heraclitus

One of these days is none of these days.
- English proverb

Would that life were like the shadow cast by a wall or a tree, but it is like the shadow of a bird in flight.
- The Talmud

A permanent state of transition is man's most noble condition.
- Juan Ramon Jimenez

If you dam a river it stagnates. Running water is beautiful water.
- English Proverb

There is nothing noble about being superior to some other men. The true nobility is in being superior to your previous self.
- Hindustani proverb

Even a clock that is not going is right twice a day.
- Polish Proverb

There is a time for departure even when there's no certain place to go.
- Tennessee Williams

Solitude / Loneliness

It is not always lonely to be alone. Quite the opposite. Solitude can be glorious. True loneliness is a product of isolation and rejection, feeling unwanted and unloved, personally impoverished. Solitude is a choice. Loneliness is not. Solitude has its companions, a full range of active senses, heightened awareness and connection to place and time, firm grounding for the feet and thin air for the soaring spirit. Solitude feels good, loneliness does not. Solitude supports creativity, loneliness breeds only discontent. Human presence even in great numbers does not immunize against loneliness. When no one cares, no one cares period. If you feel no one cares, no one cares period. The perception is the reality. Each of us reaches out to connect. That is natural. It is not enough to be an island, a solitary self in a self-sufficient world. Each of us must also reach back in to touch another reacher for all of this to work.

Language has created the word 'loneliness' to express
the pain of being alone, and the word 'solitude' to
express the glory of being alone.
-       Paul Tillich

Loneliness and the feeling of being unwanted is the
most terrible poverty.
-       Mother Teresa

I never said 'I want to be alone.' I only said, 'I want to be
left alone.' There is all the difference.
-       Greta Garbo

I never found the companion that was so companionable
as solitude.
-       Henry David Thoreau

One of the greatest necessities in America it to discover
creative solitude.
-       Carl Sandburg

On stage I make love to twenty-five thousand people;
then I go home alone.
-       Janice Joplin

The eternal quest of the individual human being is to
shatter his loneliness.
-       Norman Cousins

Honest / Dishonest

To say what you mean and mean what you say is to be honest. The truth is tough at times to tell. It can hurt. It does hurt when told in the wrong words or at the wrong time or in the wrong place. Yet in spite of the risk and challenge, honesty must serve as the common thread that unites thoughts, beliefs and deeds. We know the truth, though hard work in denying it can confuse and complicate almost to the point where facts seem fiction and fiction facts. What binds us and what we are bound to is truth and a commitment to not extinguish our inner flame or let another do the same. For each of us is her own best advertisement if we stick to what is, rather than inventing some new reality that, in the end, is never to be trusted nor valued to the same degree as was the original. Facts are facts, not to be falsified or rearranged. When we begin to falsify, to counterfeit, we run the risk of undermining our own happiness. Because true relationships are built on honest words, spoken aloud, without enlargement, without manipulation. And healthiness thrives where secrets dare not hide.

I have said what I meant and meant what I said. I have not done as well as I should have liked to have done, but I have done my best, frankly and forthrightly; no man can do more, and you are entitled to no less.

-    Adlai Stevenson

I don't give them hell. I just tell the truth and they think it is hell.

-    Harry S. Truman

There can be no happiness if the things we believe in are different from the things we do.

-    Freya Stark

Truth is not introduced into the individual from without, but was within him all the time.

-    Søren Kierkegaard

I am not bound to win, but I am bound to be true. I am not bound to succeed, but I am bound to live up to what light I have.

-    Abraham Lincoln

The best ad is a good product.

-    Alan H. Meyer

What you don't see with your eyes, don't invent with your tongue.

-    Jewish proverb

There are two kinds of statistics, the kind you look up and the kind you make up.

-    Rex Stout

Real happiness is cheap enough, yet how dearly we pay
for its counterfeit.
- Hosea Ballou

A friend is one before whom I may speak aloud.
- Ralph Waldo Emerson

And all who told it added something new
And all who heard it made enlargements too.
- Alexander Pope

You're only as sick as your secrets.
- Anon.

Creative / Regimented

Our humanity is most clearly expressed by our individual creativity. Unique ideas that spring from every spirit carry us beyond the restrictions of time and space and circumstance. They allow us to think beyond the lines of reason and along paths less traveled or never traveled before. They are a form of pleasurable groping, reaching beyond and defying perfect order. They are part of our individual becoming, of our own self-realization. These ideas, or flowing of ideas see perfect order as an unworthy goal and tolerate high levels of imperfection. They allow projection beyond the closed gate of reasoned thought or consistency. Since the ideas that arise are new, or appear new since the same may have been forgotten in another time, another space, they may expect to be opposed by common thinkers and common doers and little minds. For original ideas contradict and break the rules without apology. To be nobody but yourself be prepared to fight, and expect opposition from those who would keep you in a rut, busy, and unable to create moments of excitement out of your own dreams.

Whosoever would be a man must be a non-conformist.
-    Ralph Waldo Emerson

An idea is salvation by imagination.
-    Frank Lloyd Wright

Think sideways!
-    Edward de Bono

How do I work? I grope.
-    Albert Einstein

Perfect order is the forerunner of perfect horror.
-    Carlos Fuentes

My mother said to me, "If you become a soldier, you'll
be a general, if you become a monk, you'll end up as the
pope." Instead, I became a painter and wound up as
Picasso.
-    Pablo Picasso

Removing the faults in a stage-coach may produce a
perfect stage-coach, but it is unlikely to produce the first
motor car.
-    Edward de Bono

Consistency is the last refuge of the unimaginative.
-    Oscar Wilde

New opinions are always suspected, and usually
opposed, without any other reason but because they are
not already common.
-    John Locke

A foolish consistency is the hobgoblin of little minds, adored by statesmen and philosophers and divines. With consistency a great soul has simply nothing to do. He may as well concern himself with his shadow on the wall. Speak what you think now in hard words and tomorrow speak what tomorrow thinks in hard words again, though it contradict everything you said today.

- Ralph Waldo Emerson

To be nobody-but-yourself – in a world which is doing its best, night and day, to make you everybody else – means to fight the hardest battle which any human being can fight; and never stop fighting.

- e.e. cummings

There are those who would misteach us that to stick in a rut is consistency – and a virtue, and that to climb out of the rut is inconsistency – and a vice.

- Mark Twain

What we really mean by originality is the modification of ideas.

- Zora Neale Hurston

Extreme busyness, whether at school, or college, kirk or market, is a symptom of deficient vitality; and a faculty for idleness implies a catholic appetite and a strong sense of personal identity.

- Robert Louis Stevenson

Humble / Boastful

To be heralded at a young age is a special burden. It leaves within the honored and those who surround her a constant need to justify the award, a subtle process that can reorder an individual's priorities away from growth and exploration and toward familiar and safe terrain. Awards and recognitions always contain within the packaging inducements to see oneself as separate, distinct, superior, even when these feelings are resisted. That is why wise people are often careful to do their good under cover, in quiet ways, not out of false humility but because it ensures the full pleasure of the giving. Public displays will always be suspect.   For it can be difficult to define in each and every act the complex tangle of motivations. Is this for me or thee? Am I bragging? And if so, doesn't that take the glow out of the glowworm? Self-praise provides no credible recommendation. It is not the same as self-confidence which is essential to success. The greatness is in the smallness – that is the mystery. With the modesty comes the admiration, accepting that if the applause never comes, still the good that was done will be affirmation enough.

After I am dead, I would rather have men ask why Cato has no monument than why he had one.
- Cato the elder

The greatest monarch on the proudest throne is obliged to sit upon his own arse.
- Benjamin Franklin

The greatest pleasure I know is to do a good action by stealth, and to have it found out by accident
- Charles Lamb

Where there are no tigers, a wildcat is very self-important.
- Korean proverb

We are all worms, but I do believe that I am a glow-worm.
- Winston Churchill

Self-praise is no recommendation.
- Old saying

Do not make yourself so big. You are not so small.
- Jewish proverb

A modest man is usually admired – if people ever hear of him.
- Edgar Watson Howe

Balanced / Frenzied

Speed is not the essence. A gentle pace allows observation and learning. Nature is the great buffer, balancing back the extremes of our acids and bases, drawing life together, advancing harmony. Life is learned by modeling. All forms of life and all living are formative. We pay a price in our own development for the way we treat – positive or negative – the world and her inhabitants. To walk lightly is to listen closely to the teachings. Some may be heard, others only felt. Material needs must be fulfilled, but they alone cannot fill a person up, nor replace the sensation and penetration of beauty's presence. Look to nature and to children for your instruction and model their lessons throughout your entire life. Understand that storms must be allowed to rage and pass, that you will still be here, and the question still will be the same. "Why the haste? To what end?" You are interrelated. Trust life. Trust health. Trust yourself.

I'm a slow walker, but I never walk back.
-     Abraham Lincoln

No house should ever be on a hill, or on anything. It should be of the hill. Hill and house should live together, each the happier for the other.
-     Frank Lloyd Wright

Hurt not the earth, neither the sea, nor the trees.
-     Revelation 7:3

We have forgotten how to be good guests, how to walk lightly on the earth as other creatures do.
-     1972 Only One Earth Conference

Speak to the earth, and it shall teach thee.
-     Job 12:8

When you only have two pennies left in the world, buy a loaf of bread with one and a lily with the other.
-     Chinese proverb

Every child is an artist. The problem is how to remain an artist once he grows up.
-     Pablo Picasso

Life has to be lived – that's all there is to it. At seventy, I would say the advantage is that you take life more calmly. You know that 'this too shall pass!'
-     Eleanor Roosevelt

The more haste, the less speed.
-     John Haywood

The first law of ecology is that everything is related to everything else.

- Barry Commoner

Nature never did betray the heart that loved her.

- William Wordsworth

The first wealth is health.

- Ralph Waldo Emerson

Beauty / Ugliness

Beauty suffers by definition. There is false beauty that is superficial and short-lived as there is true beauty that is deep-seated and forever. At times these two do coexist. At times they do not. One is understated, the other overstated. One is likely to offer surprises while the other may reveal disappointments with time. One is real, the other perceived. The two have the ability to replace and displace each other. Both have the ability to distract and attract. Real beauty, from inside, creates the capacity to appreciate and absorb beauty from outside. Nature's beauty comes at shutter speed, carried on the wings of birds. If we seek the right type of beauty, it is worth great effort. But in this regard, it is worth reminding that we humans can confuse external with internal and suffer the disappointment of not finding goodness where we thought it should reside. To find the real thing, our hearts must be in the right place. If a person has beauty within, and is loved, it becomes visible on the surface, as a glow, a happiness, an ease of conversation, a comfort to another soul. Such beauty gained suffers not the dimunitions of time but rather grows each day, to the end of time, and beyond.

The ideal woman which is in every man's mind is evoked by a word or phrase or the shape of her wrist, her hand. The most beautiful description of a woman is by understatement. Remember, all Tolstoy ever said to describe Anna Karenina was that she was beautiful and could see in the dark like a cat. Every man has a different idea of what's beautiful, and it's best to take the gesture, the shadow of the branch, and let the mind create the tree.

- William Faulkner

No effort that we make to attain something beautiful is ever lost.

- Helen Keller

It is amazing how complete is the delusion that beauty is goodness.

- Leo Tolstoy

Though we travel the world over to find the beautiful, we must carry it with us or we find it not.

- Ralph Waldo Emerson

Do you love me because I'm beautiful, or am I beautiful because you love me?

- Oscar Hammerstein, II

No Spring, nor Summer beauty hath such grace,
As I have seen in one Autumnal face.

- John Donne

Have nothing in your houses that you do not know to be useful, or believe to be beautiful.

- William Morris

Grateful / Hateful

Hate hurts the hater. A burning passion self digests. When you expect too much you breed your own resentment. But if your expectations are zero, every little blessing is a pleasant and welcome surprise. Human nature wants to compare, to compete, to have and in the process create have-nots. But isn't there enough misfortune already, without creating more? Wouldn't it be better just to disengage from the battle, let go of the hate, and commit to a different future rather than the same old past? It is possible there are blessings already on the way that can't get through the veil of hate that you have hung. No one's paying attention to what has angered you but you. Letting go of hate lets you be yourself, in all your silliness and imperfection, in all your goodness and fullness. Hate degrades and diminishes you. Gratitude creates openness to blessings and the likelihood that your blessings will multiply in your sharing them with others.

To carry a grudge is like being stung to death by one bee.
- William H. Walton

Holding on to anger is like grasping a hot coal with the intent of throwing it at someone else; you are the one who gets burned.
- Buddha

When one's expectations are reduced to zero, one really appreciates everything one does have.
- Stephen Hawking

If all our misfortunes were laid in one common heap, whence every one must take equal portion, most people would be content to take their own and depart.
- Solon

We give thanks for unknown blessings already on their way.
- Sacred ritual chant

It is one of the blessings of old friends that you can afford to be stupid with them.
- Ralph Waldo Emerson

Not what we say about our blessings, but how we use them, is the true measure of our thanksgiving.
- W.T. Purkiser

Honorable / Dishonorable

Honor is to have the courage of one's own convictions, to at the end of the day, at the end of each day, be able to live with yourself. Each individual must decide for herself where to draw the line, the decision of what is right, the decision of what is wrong. To go against one's own convictions is to shirk from one's duty to self, to family, to community, to society. The seriousness of honor and dishonor is that it plays out on many levels. It is a moral duty which when disappointed affects personal happiness, disaffecting at the source. The choice of what to honor is more critical than the honoring itself. For it is quite natural for humans to willingly sacrifice their very lives in the name of honor. Yet this willingness does not automatically assure that the life was worth the taking. For humans have a unique ability to deceive themselves. A badge of honor may prove in retrospect a brand of dishonor. It is the choice then, the choice that counts, a choice of worth, a choice for all time, a choice well worth the fiery path of self-sacrifice. Receiving honors does not always equate with being honorable. The true honor is in being able to depart this world a friend to yourself.

Each man must for himself alone decide what is right and what is wrong, which course is patriotic and which isn't. You cannot shirk this and be a man. To decide against your conviction is to be an unqualified and inexcusable traitor, both to yourself and to your country, let men label you as they may.

- Mark Twain

Human happiness and moral duty are inseparably connected.

- George Washington

They were never defeated, they were only killed.

- Said of the French Foreign Legion

A thing is not necessarily true because a man dies for it.

- Oscar Wilde

The fiery trials through which we pass will light us down in honor or dishonor to the latest generation.

- Abraham Lincoln

It is better to deserve honors and not have them than to have them and not deserve them.

- Mark Twain

I desire to conduct the affairs of this administration that if at the end...I have lost every other friend on earth, I shall at least have one friend left, and that friend shall be down inside of me.

- Abraham Lincoln

Good/Evil

That there is goodness in this world is undeniable. That there is evil, capable of taking root to branch and multiply with breathtaking speed and by surprise is equally the case. ~~But little candles throw great beams, and light enlightens, while sins cast long shadows~~. We and our world are both evil and good. By our deeds you shall know us. All the learning, earning and yearning can't replace a moment's hesitation or justice withheld in the face of evil. Tyranny, poverty, disease – there is more than enough to battle to prove our inner worth. Though it's useful to remind that the knowledge and power that accrues can always be turned upon ourselves. That we possess a conscience does not assure its use. But it can be stirred by the universe and the belief that we all have a right to be here among the trees and stars. Amid the noisy confusion people do somehow find peace inside, and dreams of a beautiful world, and a confidence (sometimes shaken but never withdrawn) that injustice is a two-edged sword and given time justice will prevail.

I am as bad as the worst, but, thank God, I am as good as the best.
-     Walt Whitman

There are a thousand hacking at the branches of evil to one who is striking at the roots.
-     Henry David Thoreau

How far that little candle throws his beams! So shines a good deed in a naughty world.
-     William Shakespeare

All sins cast long shadows.
-     Irish proverb

He maketh his sun to rise on the evil and on the good, and sendeth rain on the just and on the unjust.
-     Jesus Christ

By his deeds we know a man.
-     African Proverb

There are three ingredients in the good life: learning, earning and yearning.
-     Christopher Morley

Three things are good in little measure and evil in large: yeast, salt and hesitation.
-     The Talmud

Charity is no substitute for justice withheld.
-     St. Augustine

Now the trumpet summons us again – not as a call to bear arms, though arms we need; not as a call to battle, though embattled we are; but a call to bear the burden of a long twilight struggle, year in and year out, 'rejoicing in hope, patient in tribulation', a struggle against the common enemies of man: tyranny, poverty, disease and war itself.

- John F. Kennedy

The genius of Einstein leads to Hiroshima.
- Pablo Picasso

A man's vanity tells him what is honour; a man's conscience what is justice.
- Walter Savage Landor

Beyond a wholesome discipline, be gentle with yourself. You are a child of the universe no less than the trees and the stars; you have a right to be here. And whether or not it is clear to you, no doubt the universe is unfolding as it should. Therefore be at peace with God, whatever you conceive Him to be, and whatever your labours and aspirations, in the noisy confusion of life keep peace with your soul. With all its sham, drudgery and broken dreams, it is still a beautiful world.
- From the works of Max Ehrmann

Injustice never rules forever.
- Seneca

Powerful / Powerless

What could be worse than knowing what's right and not having the power to accomplish it? How about having the power and trampling others without thought or purpose? Power is expressed by those with values, weak and strong alike. Power is as soon the companion of rudeness as goodness. Actions do discriminate while words may not. Those on the side of the good without the might, must bide their time, relying on the strength of their ideas to rise as the weakness of their opponents' ideas fall. When that time arises, the accumulated passion and strength of purpose exposes the full power and allows the idea and it's creator to prevail against opponents whose only purpose is their own self-importance. If not successful at first start, the ability to avert destruction today will make you stronger tomorrow. Tyrants are both evil and powerful. When they die, power is relinquished. Martyrs are both good and powerful. When they die, their power is enhanced.

This is the worst pain a man can suffer: to have insight into much and power over nothing.
- Herodotus

When elephants fight it is the grass that suffers.
- African saying

Rudeness is the weak man's imitation of strength.
- Eric Hoffer

If we are strong, our strength will speak for itself. If we are weak, words will be no help.
- John F. Kennedy

If you can't bite down, don't show your teeth.
- Old saying

A good indignation brings out all one's powers.
- Ralph Waldo Emerson

Most of the trouble in the world is caused by people wanting to be important.
- T. S. Eliot

What does not destroy me makes me strong.
- Friedrich Nietzsche

The tyrant dies and his rule is over; the martyr dies and his rule begins.
- Søren Kierkegaard

Open / Closed

It is a natural impulse, a protective impulse of individuals, families and societies to close ranks and erect walls. The real risk in this behavior for the individual is the limits it imposes on information exchange and personal growth. Not hearing provides momentary comfort, sparing the individual of criticism that may be painful. But openness is also a positive stimulus for growth. The family is a good place to practice openness, to reject simple mind control and intimidation, to listen to the young and old. Openness, learned inside the family, can be exercised outside the family, and be expressed as tolerance and reaching out to experience the richness of other cultures and approaches. We are all members of the human family. Democracy seeks out opposition for its balancing effect, for the discourse it provokes and the micro-revolutions it assures as a hedge against tyranny and the danger of accumulated unwanted frustrations that might be harnessed by extremists. Extremists' major danger is their fundamental intolerance directed at citizens rather than ideas. Our citizens strength is their constant personal growth, inseparable from the daily exposure to the messy, unpredictable, and surprising array of diversity. Take all this away and both sides of life look pretty much the same. Staleness sets in with weakness close behind.

Don't ever take a fence down until you know why it was put up.
> - Robert Frost

I am not so much concerned with the right of everyone to say anything he pleases as I am about our need as a self-governing people to hear everything relevant.
> - John F. Kennedy

When three people call you an ass, put on a bridle.
> - Spanish proverb

Everyone likes to think that he has done reasonably well in life, so that it comes as a shock to find our children behaving differently. The temptation is to tune them out; it takes much more courage to listen.
> - John D. Rockefeller, III

In a democracy, the opposition is not only tolerated as constitutional, but must be maintained because it is indispensable.
> - Walter Lippman

What is dangerous about extremists is not that they are extreme, but that they are intolerant. The evil is not what they say about their cause, but what they say about their opponents.
> - Robert F. Kennedy

He that has seen both sides of fifty has lived to little purpose if he has no other views of the world than he had when he was much younger.
> - William Cowper

We are now at the point where we must decide whether we are to honour the concept of a plural society which gains strength through diversity, or whether we are to have bitter fragmentation that will result in perpetual tension and strife.

-    Earl Warren

Listen / Talk

All humans desire to communicate, to express their thoughts. At the same time, all humans desire to be heard. If modeled early, talking comes naturally. Listening is an acquired skill, learned, and relearned, and relearned again. Active listening requires that you not be speaking. It's not surprising then that the best listeners choose their words carefully and in small numbers. They let others' words fill the empty space. The listening is not passive reception but supported by a full range of facial expression and body language that carry with them unique persuasive power. The problem with talking too much goes beyond its opposition to listening. Over talk is sloppy talk – too many errors, too much exaggeration, too much opportunity to say what would be better left unsaid. It is a common mistake to confuse words with knowledge. Fewer words, more carefully chosen, count more. A moment of thought prior to speaking, a little hesitation, improves speech immensely. Though hesitation may create silence, better this than noise for noise's sake. And actions, in the midst of silence, do always speak louder than words. And one last word on words, they do travel while silence stays put.

People love to talk but hate to listen. Listening is not merely not talking, though even that is beyond most of our powers; it means taking a vigorous human interest in what is being told us. You can listen like a blank wall or like a splendid auditorium where every sound comes back fuller and richer.
- Alice Duer Miller

To the good listener, half a word is enough.
- Spanish proverb

One of the best ways to persuade others is with your ears – by listening to them.
- Dean Rusk

Too much talk will include errors.
- Burmese proverb

The real art of conversation is not only to say the right thing in the right place but to leave unsaid the wrong thing at the tempting moment.
- Dorothy Nevill

He multiplieth words without knowledge.
- Job 35:16

Words should be weighed and not counted.
- Yiddish proverb

We need a reason to speak, but none to keep silent.
- Pierre Nicole

When your work speaks for itself, don't interrupt.
- Henry J. Kaiser

Whatsoever ye have spoken in darkness shall be heard in the light; and that which ye have spoken in the ear in closets shall be proclaimed upon the housetops.

-    Luke 12:13

Speaking without thinking is shooting without taking aim.

-    Spanish proverb

Humor / Humorless

There is a weightiness to the world it doesn't deserve, a heaviness that is self-imposed. Built into the human spirit, whether by Spirit or serotonin, are moments of lightness, of defiance, of resilience, of strength, released through sparkling eyes, lips curved upward, a sound distinct from reasoned words or heavy thoughts. A few in every culture have the skill to reach the hidden space in others where lives our happy defiance, and allow its contents to escape. They defy our pessimism and block it from pressing in, encroaching on our goodness. One person's release connects to another's, whose release gains entry to another's hidden space like any chemical reaction. Fast, spontaneous, creating new believers. Why not Santa Claus after all? If he would protect us. Why not laughter? If it could provide for us until perfection is assured.

I don't deserve this award, but I have arthritis and I don't deserve that either.

- Jack Benny

He deserves paradise who makes his companions laugh.

- The Koran

Laughter is the shortest distance between two people.

- Victor Borge

Angels fly because they take themselves lightly.

- G. K. Chesterton

I stopped believing in Santa Claus when I was six. Mother took me to see him in a department store and he asked for my autograph.

- Shirley Temple

Humor is my sword and my shield. It protects me. You can open a door with humor and drive a truck right through.

- Alan Simpson

God will provide – if only God would provide until he provides.

- Yiddish proverb

Courageous / Scared

When to stand firm? It's a question of judgment. One thing we know, that single individuals who resist fear, who harness its energy
and see its potential, do prevail. In the course,
they encounter resistance, most frequently
from others who have cowered to fear and
coalesced. Courage is not superhuman, but a
decision of the moment for a moment. We
think of courage as a reaction to threat, but it is
more often a creator of life – holding the line,
doing what's right, without glory, without
recognition. Courage builds in small increments, encouraging a person to go a little
farther, hold on a little longer, be a little stronger. With enough in reserve, and no other
choice, courage will suffice. Courage enhances
performance in natural response to the threat.
Determination, but not without reason, not
without the knowledge to safely advise retreat
if that is the only way to survive and fight
another day. Those who fear losing power or
being the victim of power are unlikely to
exhibit courage. Those who say they are free
of all fear are deluded. "True believers" possess a comfort which, when taken too far, may

mutate and create offensive power to be unleashed on "non-believers." History bears cautionary witness. Out of ignorance springs fear especially of the unknown. Courage is not a blunt instrument. It is informed. Tyranny is the enemy. Opinions are worth fighting for, but not at the cost of another's right to state an opposing point of view. Each person's burdens and hardships bear witness to the value of tolerance, survival and liberty.

One man with courage makes a majority.
-       Andrew Jackson

Courage is resistance to fear, mastery of fear, not absence of fear.
-       Mark Twain

There is, in addition to a courage with which men die, a courage by which men must live.
-       John F. Kennedy

We must constantly build dykes of courage to hold back the flood of fear.
-       Martin Luther King, Jr.

A wounded deer leaps the highest.
-       Emily Dickinson

My advice to you, if you should ever be in a hold up, is to line up with the cowards and save your bravery for an occasion when it may be of some benefit to you.
-       O. Henry

Fear is not an unknown emotion to us.
-       Neil Armstrong

It is not power that corrupts but fear. The fear of losing power corrupts those who wield it, and fear of the scourge of power corrupts those who object to it.
-       Aung San Suu Kui

Only the self-deceived will claim perfect freedom from fear.
-       Bill W.

Fear always springs from ignorance.
- Ralph Waldo Emerson

How much pain they have cost us, the evils which have never happened.
- Thomas Jefferson

The dogmas of the quiet past are inadequate to the stormy present. The occasion is piled high with difficulty, and we must rise with the occasion. As our case is new, so we must think anew and act anew. We must disenthrall ourselves.
- Abraham Lincoln

These are the times that try men's souls. The summer soldier and the sunshine patriot will, in this crisis, shrink from the service of their country, but he that stands it now, deserves the love and thanks of man and woman. Tyranny, like hell, is not easily conquered; yet we have this consolation with us, that the harder the conflict, the more glorious the triumph.
- Thomas Paine

Opinions cannot survive if one has no chance to fight for them
- Thomas Mann

Let every nation know, whether it wishes us well or ill, that we shall pay any price, bear any burden, meet any hardship, support any friend, oppose any foe to assure the survival and the success of liberty.
- John F. Kennedy

Generous / Selfish

You are of little help to others if you have not
first helped yourself – with knowledge,
growth, health and happiness. Generosity
flows from human warmth, not out of distance.
Those with the greatest capacity to give, share
the greatest obligation for those in need. But
since they possess unlimited capacity to produce pleasures that distract they frequently
excuse themselves the privilege of serving
others. And the punishment is to experience
life in the shallows. But for many others, of
greater and lesser means, giving, and accepting
without oppressive judgment, is natural and
feels right. They are the blessed ones.

By pursuing his own interest (the individual) frequently promotes that of the society more effectually than when he really intends to promote it. I have never known much good done by those who affected to trade for the public good.

> \- Adam Smith

Too long a sacrifice
Can make a stone of the heart.

> \- William Butler Yeats

Unto whomsoever much is given, of him shall much be required.

> \- Luke 12:48

It is customary these days to ignore what should be done in favor of what pleases us.

> \- Plautus

He who allows his day to pass by without practicing generosity and enjoying life's pleasures is like a blacksmith's bellows; he breathes, but does not live.

> \- Sanskrit proverb

Teach us to give and not to count the cost.

> \- Ignatius Loyola

To be social is to be forgiving.

> \- Robert Frost

Others / Self

In each person's life, come others who pave the way. Some are protectors, nurturers, cherishers. Others are role models, examples through whom we see not only our future selves, but also understand our fit. It's a delicate balance to value yourself enough, believe in your goodness and potential, without becoming destructively self-centered. Go too far either way and you're in trouble. Reaching outside yourself in response to others needs, not only is service, but learning. As we connect to others needs, we discover and fill our own. Both are critically important – the reaching out so that others might have a chance to reach their full potential – and the pulling back to focus on self to reach your full potential. Your self-growth allows for future greater independence and progressively less need for others' daily assistance. Self-sufficiency grows. Over time and beyond, you move from modeling to being a model yourself, as your shadow lengthens and strengthens, as you become the other to someone's future self.

No him, no me.
>   - Dizzie Gillespie
>   on Louis Armstrong

There is a magnet in your heart that will attract true friends. That magnet is unselfishness, thinking of others first. When you learn to live for others, they will live for you.
>   - Paramahansa Yogananda

To be happy, we must not be too concerned with others.
>   - Albert Camus

If a free society cannot help the many who are poor, it cannot save the few who are rich.
>   - John. F. Kennedy

The environment is everything that isn't me.
>   - Albert Einstein

Don't ask of your friends what you yourself can do.
>   - Quintus Ennius

An institution is the lengthening shadow of one man.
>   - Ralph Waldo Emerson

Reality / Perception

Reality is so real, so present, so in place that it is easily overlooked, ignored, or displaced. The human mind has a unique ability to convincingly fashion its own reality in a manner that allows a person to absolutely know what he absolutely knows not to be so. While it is true that we frequently fashion the truth to fit the surrounding environment and circumstances, it is equally true that external forces and realities help dictate reality. A threat in one setting with one individual may be a blessing to another in a different time and place. This is not to say that any one of us can change reality by simply ignoring it. But it is to say that reality is a bit soft around the edges, never quite as good or as bad as we perceive. To achieve anywhere near one's full potential or capacity requires practical consideration of reality. But this consideration rightly understands that eyes and ears can be mistaken. Not everything that is real is readily seen or heard. Nor is earnest straightforward communications delivered face to face to be confused with honesty or infused with blind confidence. For this may or may not be the case. People do lie you know. And they will do it to your face. What each of us says never fully matches what we think, feel, or believe. If that were the case, the harsh reality would leave little room for friendship. So perceptions take the place, a softer reality that supports greater commonality than may in fact exist. After all, life's not perfect. It's a predicament. On any given day, each of us may require a clean slate to tell our story anew, without prejudice.

That that is is.
                    -    Shakespeare, 'Twelfth Night'

It isn't what we don't know that gives us trouble, it's
what we know that ain't so.
                    -    Will Rogers

In the ant's house, the dew is a flood.
                    -    Old saying

Facts do not cease to exist because they are ignored.
                    -    Aldous Huxley

If I've learned anything in my seventy years it's that
nothing's as good or as bad as it appears.
                    -    Bushrod H. Campbell

One's task is not to turn the world upside down, but to
do what is necessary at the given place and with a due
consideration of reality.
                    -    Dietrich Bonhoffer

They are ill discoverers that think there is no land, when
they see nothing but sea.
                    -    Francis Bacon

I have known a vast quantity of nonsense talked about
bad men not looking you in the face. Don't trust that
conventional idea. Dishonesty will stare honesty out of
countenance, any day in the week, if there is anything to
be got by it.
                    -    Charles Dickens

If we were all given by magic the power to read each other's thoughts, I suppose the first effect would be to dissolve all the friendships.

- Bertrand Russell

Life is not a spectacle or a feast; it is a predicament.

- George Santayana

You cannot write in the chimney with charcoal.

- Russian proverb

Big Picture / Small Picture

Is it stones that make the mountain or is the mountain made of stones? To which should our attention first be drawn? There are those who say the answer is to see it all, from different points of view, before choosing to edit or ignore. After all, you have to get by the big to focus on the little. The focus is necessary, they say, to correct, or fix, or adjust the picture. The problem is that too rapid concentration on the small, and its correction, may correct for you but further distance your neighbor from a solution. That is the cost of the big picture missed. For what is big and what is small? How often does one seek the big prize, only to find, once won, that it is not so big after all? Often! And how often does one ignore the little pleasure or moment of truth only to find years later it was not so small after all? Often! In the ever present battle between the children and the grass, should play give way to a perfect carpet or the reverse? And do we not all end up in ground in the end, so why not kick up some dirt before we permanently dissolve? There are games and there are championships. There is matter that often doesn't matter and spirit that wants to slip right through the fingers so busy reaching out for something else. It is the little that makes the big. But it is the big that creates the environment for tomorrow's little. So it contradicts. Very well. Then it is all of ours to sort out.

Men trip not on mountains, they stumble on stones.
- Old saying

See everything: overlook a great deal: correct a little.
- Pope John XXIII

Many a man curses the rain that falls upon his head, and knows not that it brings abundance to drive away hunger.
- Saint Basil

My father used to play with my brother and me in the yard. Mother would come out and say, "You're tearing up the grass." "We're not raising grass," Dad would reply. "We're raising boys."
- Harmon Killebrew

A tomb now suffices him for whom the whole world was not sufficient.
- Anonymous epitaph for Alexander the Great

Set short term goals and you'll win games. Set long term goals and you'll win championships!
- Anon.

We have grasped the mystery of the atom, and rejected the Sermon on the Mount.
- Omar Bradley

The creation of a thousand forests is in one acorn.
- Ralph Waldo Emerson

The proper time to influence the character of a child is about 100 years before he is born.

> \- Dean William R. Inge

Do I contradict myself?
Very well, then I contradict myself,
I am large, I contain Multitudes.

> \- Walt Whitman

Lead / Follow

Leading is more about reaching one's full potential than subjecting one's will on to reluctant followers. To see in yourself an unmet dream, a chance to become, words to be written, deeds to be done, and to do them places you in the lead of yourself. You are neither slave nor master. You are just you. Pursuing your own potential rarely can be done in isolation. It is more commonly an immersion, a connecting, requiring many roles, and many learnings, often of the same reality examined and reexamined from different points of view. It involves blending in, not sticking out. If there is leading, it is through the force of ideas not the force of force, touching many bases, not just one. The movement toward full potential, the pathway to this point of growth is eased by those who assist, who respond to your call and provide support. The journey then is underway. The mystery is that without coercion or diminishment of any kind, the leader leaves behind a group of volunteers more willing and more likely to lead themselves.

Why should I deem myself to be a chisel, when I could be the artist?

-   J.C.F. von Schiller

As I would not be a slave, so I would not be a master. This expresses my idea of democracy.

-   Abraham Lincoln

Nobody is qualified to become a statesman who is entirely ignorant of the problems of wheat.

-   Socrates

I don't believe in just ordering people to do things. You have to sort of grab an oar and row with them.

-   Harold Geneen

We are governed not by armies and police but by ideas.

-   Mona Caird

The go-between wears out a thousand sandals.

-   Japanese proverb

The world stands aside to let anyone pass who knows where he is going.

-   David Starr Jordan

The final test of a leader is that he leaves behind in other men the conviction and the will to carry on.

-   Walter Lippman

Principled / Unprincipled

The principles most people aspire to live by come quite naturally to mind because they simply feel right, or sound right to the majority. We make choices – good over evil, love over hate, gentleness over cruelty. Individuals, families, and societies fight over principles, some say because it is simpler than living up to those principles. We equate certain virtues with success – sincerity, justice, chastity, humility, and industry to name a few. But whether this equation holds true is dependent on how we define success (long-term vs. short-term, ourselves vs. others, material vs. spiritual). Whose success are we talking about, the principled or the unprincipled? Principled people seem to feel comfortable in their own clothes. Principled people do not seem to surround themselves with unprincipled people. Principled people are viewed as valuable rather than successful. Their values are not ideas which flow from their mind, but rather are a part of a mindset. Knowing it deeply, they do it easily and naturally. They are not forced to seek direction or justification from outside because they are self-directed from within. The measure of their principles can be taken by where they spend their time and the objects they pursue. The methods matter little if grounded in principles. Because principles provide the direction and the pathway to a worthy destination.

Intelligence is derived from two words – *inter* and *legere* – *inter* meaning 'between' and *legere* meaning 'to choose'. An intelligent person, therefore, is one who has learned 'to choose between'. He knows that good is better than evil, that confidence should supersede fear, that love is superior to hate, that gentleness is better than cruelty, forbearance than intolerance, compassion than arrogance, and that truth has more virtue than ignorance.

- J. Martin Klotsche

It is often easier to fight for principles than to live up to them.

- Adlai Stevenson

Thirteen virtues necessary for true success: temperance, silence, order, resolution, frugality, industry, sincerity, justice, moderation, cleanliness, tranquility, chastity, and humility.

- Benjamin Franklin

Beware all enterprises that require new clothes.

- Henry David Thoreau

Who lies for you will lie against you.

- Bosnian proverb

Try not to become a man of success, but rather a man of value.

- Albert Einstein

A belief is not merely an idea the mind possesses; it is an idea that possesses the mind.

- Robert Bolton

Doing what's right isn't the problem. It's knowing what's right.

> - Lyndon B. Johnson

We trust, sir, that God is on our side. It is more important to know that we are on God's side.

> - Abraham Lincoln

The true worth of a man is to be measured by the objects he pursues.

> - Marcus Aurelius

The man who grasps principles can successfully select his own methods. The man who tries methods, ignoring principles, is sure to have trouble.

> - Ralph Waldo Emerson

If we are facing in the right direction, all we have to do is keep on walking.

> - Ancient Buddhist Proverb

Help / Hurt

On the surface, the decision whether to help or hurt seems remarkably clear cut. Yet, it is never as easy as it seems. First you need to recognize that someone needs help. What will be required to be effective and in what order comes next. Then collaboration, marshalling others skills to shore up those you may lack. Helping frequently requires patience and persistence. Hurting is much more immediate and easy to deliver. It only takes one person to begin to tear down, but usually multiple people, cooperating and working in concert to build up. Still helping is magnetic and partners have difficulty resisting the urge to chip in and contribute. And frequently the helper who began it all, can step back and enjoy the fact that her help has spread to the helpers themselves who can't recall who was there first because each is too involved. If you want to help, there's always an opportunity as long as you're not too selective. In the end, each time you reach out, others reach back, forming you and drawing out of you a reservoir of strength and goodness.

The meaning of good and bad, of better or worse, is simply helping or hurting.

- Ralph Waldo Emerson

Do what you can, with what you have, where you are.

- Theodore Roosevelt

Any jackass can kick down a barn, but it takes a good carpenter to build one.

- Sam Rayburn

Make happy those who are near, and those who are far will come.

- Chinese proverb

As for the best leaders, the people do not notice their existence. The next best, the people honour and praise. The next, the people fear, and the next the people hate. When the best leader's work is done, the people say, 'we did it ourselves!'

- Lao-Tzu

I am part of all that I have met.

- Alfred, Lord Tennyson

Wise / Smart

Wisdom flows from understanding. Knowledge, self-control, and service are its pillars. Wisdom informs what is worth fighting for or not. Wisdom breeds new ideas, new insights and new visions, in a way that simplifies and transmits understanding. Wisdom and maturation are allies. Time carries suffering and hardship, which unleashes insight and growth. With maturity the wise learn patience, trust, confidence and timing. Shadows of fear and blind alleys of indecision and complexity are avoided, leaving only the lessons, only the learnings to linger within the heart.

A wise and an understanding heart.
-    1 Kings 3:12

Surely the shortest commencement address in history –
and for me one of the most memorable – was that of Dr.
Harold E. Hyde, president of New Hampshire's Ply-
mouth State College. He reduced his message to the
graduating class to these three ideals: 'Know yourself –
Socrates. Control yourself – Cicero; Give yourself –
Christ.'
-    Walter T. Tatara

It is said that a wise man who stands firm is a statesman,
and a foolish man who stands firm is a catastrophe.
-    Adlai Stevenson

Only the wise possess ideas, the greater part of mankind
are possessed by them.
-    Samuel Taylor Coleridge

Knowledge is a process of piling up facts; wisdom lies in
their simplification.
-    Martin H. Fisher

Wisdom comes only through suffering.
-    Aeschylus

It is characteristic of wisdom not to do desperate things.
-    Henry David Thoreau

We should be careful to get out of an experience only the wisdom that is in it – and stop there, lest we be like the cat that sits down on a hot stove lid. She will never sit down on a hot stove-lid again – and that is well; but also she will never sit down on a cool one anymore.

-    Mark Twain

Knowledge comes, but wisdom lingers.

-    Alfred, Lord Tennyson

Let my heart be wise. It is the gods' best gift.

-    Euripides

Intimate / Impersonal

To have enough inside to give away is not
enough. For it is not the same as the giving
itself. To allow oneself to soar, in moments of
revelry, risks a fall, an injury. We all know that.
But to pull back, to self-protect, means losing
what the person hopes to save. Barriers once
constructed, grow taller but no more protective. And they offend our instincts, our nature
to have our hearts reach out. Each woman,
each man is a person worth meeting, greeting,
knowing, loving. Each has worth, value,
goodness. Each deserves comfort, touch and
intimacy. To lose the ability to connect with
other persons, to become impersonal is doubly
regressive. First you lose the hearts and souls
of the relations, and second you suffer the self-
recrimination of recognizing the deafening and
deadening of your own spirit.

To make a prairie it takes clover and one bee
one clover, and a bee,
and revelry
the revelry alone will do,
if bees are few.

-       Emily Dickinson

We are adhering to life now with our last muscle – the
heart.

-       Djuna Barnes

Advice to young writers who want to get ahead without
annoying delays: don't write about Man, write about a
man.

-       E. B. White

I feel bad that I don't feel worse.

-       Michael Frayn

Confident / Insecure

To believe in yourself is to believe in your self –
your uniqueness, your special view of the
world, your difference, the place you fill today,
the space you will fill tomorrow. You are you.
Who else can make that claim? No other has
the right to diminish you. You are in control.
If you let your head hang, it's your neck going
loose – not someone pushing down – to fault.
The first friend and most important one to you
is you. So go gentle on the criticism. Don't
exaggerate your faults. To believe in yourself,
you must approve of yourself. Who's going to
vote for you, if you won't vote for yourself? If
you value yourself, so will others. If you say
and believe you're inferior, you are; if you say
and believe you're not, you're not. It's as
simple as that. Drop the dread. Drop it now.
The longer you hold on, the more damage
done. Drop the fear of the unknown, chasing
someone else's dreams, illusions that were
never really yours anyway. Accept the unknown. You're a candle to be lit. There are
rooms out there for you to light up. Everybody
and everything has problems built in. You just
can't see them because they are so well hidden.

You don't know what others say to themselves in their private prayers. There's only one person who can lick you. That's you. But there are many people who will love you, if first you'll love yourself.

If I try to be like him, who will be like me?
-	Yiddish proverb

Every man who attacks my belief diminishes in some degree my confidence in it, and therefore makes me uneasy, and I am angry with him who makes me uneasy.
-	Samuel Johnson

Never let your head hang down. Never give up and sit down and grieve. Find another way. And don't pray when it rains if you don't pray when the sun shines.
-	Satchel Paige

Be a friend to thyself and others will be so too.
-	Thomas Fuller

Never exaggerate your faults; your friends will attend to that.
-	Robert C. Edwards

A man cannot be comfortable without his own approval
-	Mark Twain

If you really do put a small value upon yourself, rest assured the world will not raise your price.
-	Anon.

No one can make you feel inferior without your consent.
-	Eleanor Roosevelt

I've developed a new philosophy – I only dread one day at a time.
-	Charles M. Schulz

The longer we dwell on our misfortunes, the greater is their power to harm us.
-   Voltaire

The unknown is what it is. And to be frightened of it is what sends everybody scurrying around chasing dreams, illusions, wars, peace, love, hate, all that. Unknown is what it is. Accept that it's unknown, and it's plain sailing.
-   John Lennon

Neither do we light a candle and put it under a bushel, but on a candlestick; and it giveth light unto all that are in the house.
-   Matthew 5:15

People are crying up the rich and variegated plumage of the peacock, and he is himself blushing at the sight of his ugly feet.
-   Sa'Di

There are few men who dare to publish to the world the prayers they make to Almighty God.
-   Montaigne

I have seen boys on my baseball team go into slumps and never come out of them, and I have seen others snap right out and come back better than ever. I guess more players lick themselves than are ever licked by an opposing team. The first thing any man has to know is how to handle himself.
-   Connie Mack

Reflective / Reactive

Reflection moves along the time line with ease. Varying from one individual to the next, time in past, present and future defines regret, remorse, anger, joy, hope, and plans for one's future self. At its best, reflection allows the individual to learn from past experiences, improve present performance and behavior, and steer toward a future better self. To plan ahead demands the capacity for self reflection which requires courage and the belief that you can help shape your own environment. In contrast, reacting to an ever-changing environment is taking the easy way out. Wait for troubles to arise, for threats to materialize, for others to take the risk to lead, and then react when and if there is no other choice. In a rapidly changing environment, reacting and reflecting merge, as the speed and weight of critical events converge and demand immediate response. Delay at all, and the opportunity is lost. Commit to plan, to lead, to be aware of your surroundings and their context. The answers, the plan, the decisions will come from within. The mind is only able to think and instruct with a single voice. But it will resist enslavement to external forces. Reflect and you will be open and free.

When the mind is thinking, it is talking to itself.
-     Plato

Have the courage to act instead of react.
-     Earlene Larson Jenks

A life of reaction is a life of slavery, intellectually and spiritually. One must fight for a life of action, not reaction.
-     Rita Mae Brown

The man who has no inner life is the slave of his surroundings.
-     Henri Frederic Amiel

I claim not to have controlled events, but confess plainly that events have controlled me.
-     Abraham Lincoln

If you fail to plan, you plan to fail.
-     Old saying

In the main it is not by introspection but by reflecting on our living in common with others that we come to know ourselves. What is revealed? It is an original creation. Freely the subject makes himself what he is, never in this life is the making finished, always it is in process, always it is a precarious achievement that can slip and fall and shatter.
-     Bernard Lonergan

Many men go fishing all of their lives without knowing that it is not fish they are after.
-     Henry David Thoreau

Smart / Lucky

To be lucky, you have to be in the right place at the right time, and in the right state of preparedness. Being prepared is not the same as being smart. There will always be someone smarter than you. Being prepared is more about being smart enough – smart enough to recognize potential opportunity, smart enough to presume questions and circumstances , smart enough to be ready to respond. Luck is rarely passive. It happens most to those whose experiences immerse them in the complex world of people, places, problems, and failure masked as opportunity. It's hard to get lucky if you frustrate easily. It's all about alignment. Oversteering, forcing, demanding – these are not the traits found among the lucky. Preparedness, receptivity, and alertness – these are the qualities that make luck more likely. Pure luckiness is a rare phenomenon and not worth much because it is so fickle.

Luck is a matter of preparation meeting opportunity.
- Oprah Winfrey

I've had a lot of experience with people smarter than I am.
- Gerald Ford

I'm a great believer in luck, and I find the harder I work, the more I have of it.
- Thomas Jefferson

I am persuaded that luck and timing have, in my case, been very important.
- Mike Wallace

Get as much experience as you can, so that you're ready when luck works. That's the luck.
- Henry Fonda

When Ty Cobb got on first base he had an apparently nervous habit of kicking the bag… by kicking the bag hard enough Cobb could move it a full two inches closer to second base. He figured that this improved his chances for a steal, or for reaching second base safely on a hit.
- Norman Vincent Peale

Fortune brings in some boats that are not steered.
- Shakespeare, 'Cymbeline'

Fortune is fickle and soon asks back what he has given.
- Latin proverb

Action / Inaction

Movement creates its own momentum. And "thinking it" is not nearly as powerful as "doing it." Nor is "wishing it" the same as getting it done, neither for the doer or for the person for whom it is done. Failure is insignificant unless the risk is lethal. For in the failing you will find tightly packaged the learning. So gather enough information from which to launch, but not so much to become encumbered, paralyzed and have the moment lost. Indecision carries risk as well. The most difficult part is to begin. The first step sets the environment in motion and all that remains is simply alignment. Words, good intentions, promises unkept, absent deeds, these are worse than nothing. For they raise expectations, our own included, and in their deflation heighten the failure and expose the bearer to the full weight of crushing impotency. Doers stand out not for the brilliance of what is done but for their courage in stepping into the unknown, in daring to lead and mark the way for others, who in seeing it done, might find the inner strength to take their first steps. Those who consistently go first, earn the right to send another on his way. Better to fail strongly than to succeed weakly! For good intentions never get the job done. And indecision is simply that. Strength is in driving the momentum, creating new realities, while others are left to pick and choose from old discarded options.

There are risks and costs to a program of action. But they are far less than the long-range risks and costs of comfortable inaction.

- John F. Kennedy

I am not built for academic writings. Action is my domain.

- Gandhi

If a friend is in trouble, don't annoy him by asking if there is anything you can do. Think up something appropriate and do it.

- Edgar Watson Howe

It is common sense to take a method and try it. If it fails, admit it frankly and try another, but above all, try something.

- Franklin D. Roosevelt

There comes a time when you've got to say, "Let's get off our asses and go…" I have always found that if I move with 75 percent or more of the facts I usually never regret it. It's the guys who wait to have everything perfect that drive you crazy.

- Lee Iacocca

Even if you're on the right track, you'll get run over if you just sit there.

- Will Rogers

He who is outside the door has already a good part of his journey behind him.

- Dutch Proverb

If deeds are wanting, all words appear mere vanity and emptiness.

- Greek Proverb

After all is said and done, more is said than done.

- Anon.

If you want a thing done, go – if not, send.

- Benjamin Franklin

I'd rather be strongly wrong than weakly right.

- Tallulah Bankhead

Deliberate often – decide once.

- Latin proverb

It is the characteristic excellence of a strong man that he can bring momentous issues to the fore and make a decision about them. The weak are always forced to decide between alternatives they have not chosen themselves.

- Dietrich Bonhoffer

Individual / Collective

The role of the collective or community of people is determined by the needs of the people. What the individual cannot do for himself or cannot do as well by himself should beg the question "Can we help?" This is a question, not a knee-jerk response. For attempts to help may be ill-conceived and not contribute positively in part because they can disrupt individual initiative and ingenuity. This is in no way to dispute that we are members of one another, sharing a common responsibility. But the power of single individuals to rise to the occasion is awesome, and demands at times, that the occasion be allowed to arrive. As rugged as individuals are, so too are they fragile. They are joined for strength, for truth, for beauty, for adventure, for art and for peace! The most successful unions are never the product of tyranny but rather the offspring of free consent. As such they are self-governing and invite the active participation of each individual in the pursuit of reason and justice. When the collective is successful, so should be the individual, in an environment of peace and security. The efforts are both practical and theoretical, impacting individual lives and the environment that sustains them. Success requires open dialogue, debate, and decisions. The conversation defines the scope of the community, which may be as small as two neighbors planning this Saturday's school event or as large and global as modern E-nets provide. And when the collective overreaches, overpromises, overrides by arrogance the richness and diversity of the individual experience, it is art that reminds us of the sensibility, faithfulness and vision of the individual mind, and our need to ensure its supremacy. What to give up, and what to retain, in the interest of the one, in the interest of the many, will always be a question that challenges all mankind.

That government is best which governs least, because its people discipline themselves.
-       Thomas Jefferson

We are members one of another.
-       Ephesians 4:25

It is possible for a single individual to defy the whole might of an unjust empire to save his honour, his religion, his soul, and lay the foundation for that empire's fall or for its regeneration.
-       Gandhi

Snowflakes are one of natures' most fragile things, but just look what they can do when they stick together.
-       Vesta M. Kelly

A civilized society is one that exhibits the five qualities of truth, beauty, adventure, art and peace.
-       Alfred North Whitehead

True jazz is an art of individual assertion within and against the group.
-       Ralph Ellison

Democracy is based on the conviction that man has the moral and intellectual capacity, as well as the inalienable right, to govern himself with reason and justice.
-       Harry S. Truman

I respect kindness in human beings first of all, and kindness to animals. I don't respect the law; I have a total irreverence for anything connected with society except that which makes the roads safer, the beer stronger, the food cheaper and the old men and women warmer in the winter and happier in the summer.

- Brendan Behan

Every man wishes to pursue his occupation and to enjoy the fruits of his labours and the produce of his property in peace and safety, and with the least possible expense. When these things are accomplished, all the objects for which government ought to be established are answered.

- Thomas Jefferson

If you want to understand democracy, spend less time in the library with Plato, and more time in the buses with people.

- Simeon Strunsky

The job of a citizen is to keep his mouth open.

- Gunter Grass

The new electronic interdependence recreates the world in the image of a global village.

- Marshall McLuhan

When power leads man towards arrogance, poetry reminds him of his limitations. When power narrows the areas of man's concern, poetry reminds him of the richness and diversity of his experience. When power corrupts, poetry cleanses...The artist...faithful to his personal vision of reality, becomes the last champion of the individual mind and sensibility against an intrusive society and an offensive state.

- John F. Kennedy

Give / Receive

What is the point of privilege? More privilege or giving back? To which do we attach honor? Giving blesses twice again, to the giver and the receiver. You can manage success by pulling in, but values are expressed in the putting out. After the having of wealth, what else is there to do but figure out how to use it wisely, how to breed happiness? In all, there is a need to give, as in all there is a need to receive the mercy of others. Giving to a need makes you necessary. So when asked, it is wise at least, to consider responding.

People of privilege will always risk their complete destruction rather than surrender any material part of their advantage.

-   J. K. Galbraith

No person was ever honored for what he received. Honor has been the reward for what he gave.

-   Calvin Coolidge

To have great poets there must be great audiences too.

-   Walt Whitman

A successful man is he who receives a great deal from his fellow men, usually incomparably more than corresponds to his service to them. The value of a man, however, should be seen in what he gives and not in what he is able to receive.

-   Albert Einstein

I was born into it and there was nothing I could do about it. It was there, like air or food, or any other element. The only question with wealth is what you do with it.

-   John D. Rockefeller, Jr.

Should not the giver be thankful that the receiver received? Is not giving a need? Is not receiving, mercy?

-   Friedrich Nietzsche

Make yourself necessary to somebody.

-   Ralph Waldo Emerson

Many things are lost for want of asking.

-   English Proverb

Dream / Focus

We all need a place to get away, if not in our dreams then somewhere else. Imagination is not the sole province of the young but a talent for all ages. Within these musings can be found each person's longings, a reaching out for purpose and significance. Once attained, the wish becomes the truth, no longer the product for dreams. For dreams are of the future, not the present or the past. Roots are roots, and wings are wings. Dreams should not be about escaping, used as an excuse to avoid dealing with reality, or to imagine perfection or contentment in worlds less perfect than the one we inhabit. To think of that all day is to make a life out of nothing. There is a time for dreaming and a time for focusing down with constancy of purpose, concentrating one's resources and energy on the challenge of the day, not doing two things at once but doing one thing at once. Doing today without trying to do yesterday and tomorrow as companions. But while the jobs are getting done, leave time each day to dream a little, to keep alive the big ideas, so fragile and so easy to dismiss.

Those who lose dreaming are lost.
-     Australian Aboriginal proverb

Imagination grows by exercise, and contrary to common belief, is more powerful in the mature than in the young.
-     W. Somerset Maugham

The significance in a man is not what he attains but rather what he longs to attain.
-     Kahlil Gibran

There are only two lasting bequests we can hope to give our children. One of these is roots, the other, wings.
-     Hodding Carter

A child on a farm sees a plane fly overhead and dreams of a faraway place. A traveler on the plane sees the farmhouse and dreams of home.
-     Carl Burns

The secret of success is constancy to purpose.
-     Benjamin Franklin

The wise man puts all his eggs in one basket and watches the basket.
-     Andrew Carnegie

Big ideas are so hard to recognize, so fragile, so easy to kill. Don't forget that, all of you who don't have them.
-     John Elliott, Jr.

You can't think and hit at the same time.
-     Yogi Berra

Ordinary / Extraordinary

What a person considers extraordinary is a product of what each of us considers to be "the best." Awards from others do not replace one from yourself. If in your mind or heart, your effort or another's is extraordinary, then it is. We are better at judging this in others than in ourselves, tending to undervalue as ordinary our efforts or contributions that are something more. Perfection? Maybe not. But more than ordinary, and worth noting with some personal satisfaction only to reinforce it in ourselves, to say, the middle of the road is not good enough, why not the best from me? When we do something fine, it outlives our immediate presence, taking on a life of its own. Do the best you can each day. That's the way to sleep soundly each night without regrets. Greatness emerges when we are most unaware, in ordinary places on ordinary days from ordinary people through deeds, or words, or noble suffering. People rise to greatness in response to events that (for many different reasons – hesitation, fear, paralysis) have not yet drawn a response. People rise to greatness by arriving first, not out of competition but by instinct, an instinct of which they are dimly aware. For deep inside, on the border of the conscious and the unconscious, there are those who know that they were born for greatness, born to fly a little higher if not today, then perhaps tomorrow, if not in this world, then perhaps in the next.

I am easily satisfied with the very best.
- Winston Churchill

Ask many of us who are disabled what we would like in life and you would be surprised how few would say, 'Not to be disabled.' We accept our limitations.
- Itzhak Perlman

A man does not have to be an angel to be a saint.
- Albert Schweitzer

The middle of the road is where the white line is, and that's the worst place to drive.
- Robert Frost

If you aren't going all the way, why go at all?
- Joe Namath

The best effect of fine persons is felt after we have left their presence.
- Ralph Waldo Emerson

I come to the office each morning and stay for long hours doing what has to be done to the best of my ability. And when you've done the best you can, you can't do any better. So when I go to sleep I turn everything over to the Lord and forget it.
- Harry S. Truman

Men achieve certain greatness unawares, when working to another aim.
- Ralph Waldo Emerson

Not a day passes over the earth, but men and women of no note do great deeds, speak great words and suffer noble sorrows.
-    Charles Reade

The biggest things are always the easiest to do because there is no competition.
-    William Van Horne

Once you say you are going to settle for second, that's what happens to you in life, I find.
-    John F. Kennedy

If you would hit the mark, you must aim a little above it. Every arrow that flies feels the attraction of earth.
-    Henry Wadsworth Longfellow

Either you reach a higher point today, or you exercise your strength in order to be able to climb higher tomorrow.
-    Friedrich Nietzsche

Want / Need

Happiness does not reside with wants expressed or needs fulfilled. Wants may be very small or very large. What you pursue is a need, it is essential, it has a purpose beyond the simple expressed desire of wanting. After all, we all want a lot of things on any day at any moment. To want to be the greatest hitter in baseball doesn't mean you will be. People want to do things simply because they do. Justifications aren't required unless someone else is paying the bill or there is a real or potential harm involved. Needs are indispensable and few. Wants can encumber and hinder our movement toward fulfillment and disorder our priorities. The mink needs its coat, but do you? And if you had it would it really bring the pleasure it does the mink herself? The ordinary may be simple but at least it's true. Wanting expands the appetite without enlarging the meal, ensuring satisfaction will be less and less likely. And in the pursuing, innocence is lost as compromises must be made. Humans want success and happiness. That is fine. The problem comes in the definitions that define the give and take.

Before we set our hearts too much upon anything, let us examine how happy they are, who already possess it.
-     La Rochefoucauld

All I want out of life is that when I walk down the street, folks will say, "There goes the greatest hitter who ever lived."
-     Ted Williams

I want to do it because I want to do it.
-     Amelia Earhart

Most of the luxuries, and many of the so-called comforts, of life are not only not indispensable, but positive hindrances to the elevation of mankind.
-     Henry David Thoreau

No one in this world needs a mink coat but a mink.
-     Anon.

A person buying ordinary products in a supermarket is in touch with his deepest emotions.
-     John Kenneth Galbraith

Riches enlarge, rather than satisfy appetites.
-     Thomas Fuller

He that maketh haste to be rich shall not be innocent.
-     Proverbs 28:20

Wealth… and poverty: the one is the parent of luxury and indolence, and the other of meanness and vicious- ness, and both of discontent.
-     Plato

Success / Failure

Every person seems to have her own formula
for success. For success takes on as many forms
and features as there are creatures on this
earth. My success is not yours, nor should it be
since I am me and you are you. But whatever
is your measure, ability and good fortune,
persistence makes more likely your success.
Failure marks each and every path. And too
much success too quickly has destroyed men
even as they smiled and rejoiced. For undeserved, doesn't success have the right to say,
"What then makes you deserved?" Creating
laughter. Earning another's respect, a child's
love, a critic's grudging approval. Endured
betrayals. Beauty appreciated. A healthy child
made by you. A land enriched by you. A
social ill repaired by you. One life the better
because of you. A good name established and
maintained. Being right more than wrong.
Grandchildren who run to greet. Friends who
lean on you. Doing your best is fine, but if the
problem remains, is that the best you can do?
Is it possible to believe that you might find the
strength to rise after every fall, that you might
stride with strength while surrounded by
weakness, that you might sow what you reap?
It is.

Success is that old ABC – ability, breaks and courage.
- Charles Luckman

You always pass failure on the way to success.
- Mickey Rooney

Success has made failures of many men.
- Cindy Adams

Success is going from failure to failure without loss of enthusiasm.
- Sir Winston Churchill

To laugh often and much; To win the respect of intelligent people, and the affection of children; To earn the appreciation of honest critics, and endure the betrayal of false friends; To appreciate beauty; To find the best in others; To leave the world a bit better, whether by a healthy child, a garden patch, or a redeemed social condition; To know that even one life has breathed easier because you lived. This is to have succeeded.
- Ralph Waldo Emerson

If you have a good name, if you are right more often than you are wrong, if your children respect you, if your grandchildren are glad to see you, if your friends can count on you and you can count on them in time of trouble, if you can face your God and say, "I have done my best," then you are a success.
- Ann Landers

It is no use saying, 'we are doing our best.' You have got to succeed in doing what is necessary.
- Sir Winston Churchill

If I had known what it would be like to have it all, I might have been willing to settle for less.

- Lily Tomlin

Inside of a ring or out, ain't nothing wrong with going down. It's staying down that's wrong.

- Muhammad Ali

If you always live with those who are lame, you will yourself learn to limp.

- Latin Proverb

Be not deceived; God is not mocked: for whatsoever a man soweth, that shall he also reap.

- Galatians 6:7

Progress / Retreat

Progress occurs in small steps not in large. A few more moving forward then backward, in any one day, or year, or decade is cause for hope. To expect never to be reversed is unrealistic. After all people retrench and retreat with near the frequency as they advance and still manage to strike out anew. It's important though, if humans are to maintain their optimism, that in the end, in the net, forward overcomes backward. Progress requires risk, the risk of trying something new. Progress seekers try to change the world and sometimes succeed. They do not comply, relent or agree but dissent and gradually nudge against the static force. When the force responds by pushing back, they may decide to yield. For yielding eliminates the risk of no return and sure defeat. Progress requires tactics, sometimes go around, sometimes through proves best to get your way. Adaptability and good sense determine when to take advantage and when to give advantage away. For progress sometimes can occur in full retreat knowing that fighting the battle would lose the war and avoiding the battle could secure the ultimate prize.

A thousand things advance, nine hundred and ninety-nine retreat; that is progress.

- Henri Frederic Amiel

Behold the turtle. He makes progress only when he sticks his head out.

- James Bryant Conant

The reasonable man adapts himself to the world; the unreasonable one persists in trying to adapt the world to himself. Therefore all progress depends upon the unreasonable man.

- George Bernard Shaw

As the soft yield of water cleaves obstinate stone, so to yield with life solves the insolvable; to yield, I have learned, is to come back again.

- Lao-tzu

The only way round is through.

- Robert Frost

Next to knowing when to seize an opportunity, the most important thing in life is to know when to forgo an advantage.

- Benjamin Disraeli

Part of the happiness of life consists not in fighting battles, but in avoiding them. A masterly retreat is in itself a victory.

- Norman Vincent Peale

Rest / Restless

Rest is more than meets the shuttered eye. It is the shuttered eye. It is the great counter-balance for labor, pain and discontent. It is the promise of a fresh start, a second chance with each new day. It is fullness, not absence, more a filling of reserves than shedding of responsibility. Just like labor, rest deserves our careful consideration and for many it is the greater challenge – how to relax, enjoy, refresh, stay young. Rest is one pillar of a body's rhythm, a marker between day and night, a measure between work and not work. Spare moments are precious but can be wasted on the unappreciative. The appreciation comes in measure to the work it interrupts. To relax begs the reasonable question, "Relax from what?" If not from something true and worthwhile, from something that required effort, is the rest required or deserved? Good rest and good work make a peaceful death at last a lovely recognition. The restless may travel far to service discontent, to find themselves only in the end at home where the journey began. Lie down. Cool down. Rest easy. And if possible drag rest out a little longer than you think you should.

Sleep that knits up the raveled sleeve of care,
The death of each day's life, sore labour's bath,
Balm of hurt minds, great nature's second course, chief
nourisher in life's feast.

> \- Shakespeare, 'Macbeth'

To be able to fill leisure intelligently is the last product of
civilization.

> \- Arnold Toynbee

Each morning sees some task begun
Each evening sees it close.
Something attempted, something done,
Has earned a night's repose.

> \- Henry Wadsworth Longfellow

I hope to work, support my children and die quietly
without pain.

> \- Sean Connery

A man travels the world in search of what he needs and
returns home to find it.

> \- George Moore

One -If your stomach disputes you, lie down and think
cool thoughts. Two - Keep the juices flowing by jangling
around gently as you move. Three - Go very lightly on
the vices such as carrying on in society. The social
ramble ain't restful.

> \- Satchel Paige

How beautiful it is to do nothing, and then rest afterwards.

> \- Spanish proverb

Nonviolent / Violent

When entering battle against an evil foe, one
should be fortified and well-armed. The battle
can be engaged directly, weapons against
weapons, and in this case the victory goes to
the more prepared in arms and skills. But
history has proven just as often that good
people, who stand for what is right and solidly
resist what is wrong, have power to oppose, to
strike and heal in single measure through some
mysterious nonviolent conversion. If we
humans are prejudiced toward war, we are
equally prejudiced toward peace. We know
the price of violence, and its unequal tool on
our most vulnerable – the young, the poor, and
poorly educated. We know as well, that after
the embers of fiery violence slowly fade, goodness will be discovered, alive and dead, on
both sides. But dead men are forever gone.
They cannot be recovered. The sacrifice complete, is one-way, no return. So if you are to go
that way, be sure it's worth it, that no other
method can provide. What we battle for is
conquest and control of outer things. What we
sacrifice and sometimes lose forever are inner
things. Was it worth it? Sometimes yes, some-

times no. Violence does violence to both winner and loser. We are what we become. So be cautious. To paraphrase one soul, better to plan than plot, better to build and bind than burn and bomb, better to love than hate, better to advance the cause of justice than trap us in an unjust status quo. Violence is at times required, but not with the frequency we use it. Non-violence can be equally powerful and just but not without practice.

Nonviolence is the greatest force at the disposal of mankind. It is mightier than the mightiest weapon of destruction devised by the ingenuity of man.
-      Gandhi

Non-violence is a powerful and just weapon. It is a weapon unique in history, which cuts without wounding and ennobles the man who wields it. It is a sword that heals.
-      Martin Luther King, Jr.

When the rich wage war, it's the poor who die.
-      Jean-Paul Sartre

What the hell difference does it make, left or right? There were good men lost on both sides.
-      Brendan Behan

War would end if the dead could return.
-      Stanley Baldwin

The world would be a safer place,
If someone had a plan, before exploring Outer Space,
To find the Inner Man.
-      E.Y. Harburg

Whoso sheddeth man's blood, by man shall his blood be shed.
-      Genesis 9:6

When evil men plot, good men must plan. When evil men burn and bomb, good men must build and bind. When evil men shout ugly words of hatred, good men must commit themselves to the glories of love. When evil men would seek to perpetuate an unjust status quo, good men must seek to bring into being a real order of justice.

- Martin Luther King, Jr.

Nonviolence and cowardice are contradictory terms. Nonviolence is the greatest virtue, cowardice the greatest vice. Nonviolence springs from love, cowardice from hate. Nonviolence always suffers, cowardice would always inflict suffering. Perfect nonviolence is the highest bravery. Nonviolent conduct is never demoralizing, cowardice always is.

- Gandhi

Endure / Give In

How far you go in reaching your full potential is often a function of how long you last. Moving from what you are to what you could be is an extended travel. Rewards come to those who not only aspire but strive as well. Toiling upward, ever upward, is not easy but it can be satisfying. The work is made easier by the realization that there are others, past and present, who have paved the way for you, just as your labor will light the way for future travelers. Endurance, persistence, relentless efforts giving way only when good sense or honor directs, knowing that what separates each of us in the end is tipping the scale slightly from sinner to saint. That you will fall along the way is certain. Whether you will get back up is your choice and yours alone. If you do not, all the talent, genius and education in the world will not repair. Average people rise up every day and make a difference because they absolutely make the choice that failure will not be the final mark on their life's sentence. Tenacity times ten.

To be somebody you must last.
-     Ruth Gordon

It is a long road from conception to completion.
-     Moliere

We can always redeem the man who aspires and strives.
-     Goethe

The heights by me reached and kept
Were not attained by sudden flight,
But they, while their companions slept,
Were toiling upward in the night.
-     Henry Wadsworth Longfellow

Behold, we count them happy which endure. Ye have
heard of the patience of Job.
-     James 5:3

A hundred times every day I remind myself that my
inner and outer life depend on the labours of other men,
living and dead, and that I must exert myself in order to
give in the same measure as I have received.
-     Albert Einstein

Never give in, never give in, never, never, never, never –
in nothing great or small, large or petty – never give in
except to convictions of honour and good sense.
-     Winston Churchill

The Saints are the Sinners who keep on trying.
-     Robert Louis Stevenson

Fall seven times, stand up eight.
-       Japanese proverb

Nothing in the world will take the place of persistence.
Talent will not; nothing is more common than
unsuccessful men of talent. Genius will not; unrewarded
genius is almost a proverb. Education will not; the world
is full of educated derelicts. Persistence and
determination alone are omnipotent.
-       Calvin Coolidge

I am only an average man, but, by George, I work harder
at it than the average man.
-       Theodore Roosevelt

When I was a young man I observed that nine out of ten
things I did were failures. I didn't want to be a failure, so
I did ten times more work.
-       George Bernard Shaw

Let me tell you the secret that has led me to my goal. My
strength lies solely in my tenacity.
-       Louis Pasteur

Explore / Fear

Without justification, without reason, without form and boundaries, fear paralyzes individuals, communities and societies. Fear may be conquered if addressed. Picturing it, placing it on the table where it can be observed and analyzed helps. Fear can be reasoned with. Fear is often tangled up in our private affairs, tangled in strategies of avoidance, repressed but never out of sight. Running away does not help. Fear drives you in the wrong direction and is there to greet you when you arrive. Conquering fear requires that you embrace change, discarding the old, adapting to the new. In return comes comfort in playing many parts and exploring many roles. As we stretch to transform, we are brand new and fear loses its grip. Comfort develops with the experiment, and the experiment is you. It is happiness, but happiness of a different kind each time. Security is surrendered voluntarily and the hold your enemy had on you, the knowledge of what frightened you, is no longer useful to him, because it frightens you no more. You are out the door, exploring another room, one that shows no respect for fear. If you fail, so what? Most worries are short-lived. You are on the move, discovering new lands, leaving behind shores that never protected you anyway. Is it a crisis, the danger? Or an opportunity?

So let me assert my firm belief that the only thing we have to fear is fear itself – nameless, unreasoning, unjustified terror which paralyzes efforts to convert retreat into advance.

> \- Franklin D. Roosevelt

The only way to get rid of my fears is to make films about them.

> \- Alfred Hitchcock

Never let the future disturb you. You will meet it, if you have to, with the same weapons of reason which today arm you against the present.

> \- Marcus Aurelius

All men should strive to learn before they die
What they are running from, and to, and why.

> \- James Thurber

Security can only be achieved through constant change, through discarding old ideas that have outlived their usefulness and adapting others to current facts.

> \- William O. Douglas

All the world's a stage.
And all the men and women merely players.
They have their exits and their entrances,
And one man in his time plays many parts.

> \- Shakespeare, 'As You Like It'

Man's mind stretched to a new idea never goes back to its original shape.

> \- Oliver Wendell Holmes

Do not be too timid and squeamish... All life is an experiment. The more experiments you make, the better.
- Ralph Waldo Emerson

The art of living does not consist in preserving and clinging to a particular mode of happiness, but in allowing happiness to change its form without being disappointed by the change; happiness, like a child, must be allowed to grow up.
- Charles L. Morgan

Growth demands a temporary surrender of security.
- Gail Sheehy

You can discover what your enemy fears most by observing the means he uses to frighten you.
- Eric Hoffer

When one door of happiness closes, another opens; but often we look so long at the closed door that we do not see the one which has been opened.
- Helen Keller

Nothing is more despicable than respect based on fear.
- Albert Camus

One doesn't discover new lands without consenting to lose sight of the shore for a very long time.
- Andre Gide

In Chinese, the word for crisis is *wei ji*, which means danger, and *ji*, which means opportunity.
- Jan Wong

Future / Past

To be committed to the future means to be committed to a world you cannot see. To make the chore more challenging, it is difficult to see where the growth will come, both good and bad. If we could see it would be a simple chore to squish the bad seed and nurture the good. But absent the ability to predict we are left to live our lives in one-day increments, knowing that this afternoon we will know more than we did this morning. The future will arrive without our prodding, without our overplanning for a rainy day. And to dwell on an imagined tomorrow almost always compromises our handling of today. The best we can do is consider the lessons of the past and see if they apply to present circumstances. We live forward, but understand backward, turning to the older, the wiser, to stories and tales, taking only what will help, not dwelling on the grief of past losses and mistakes, not passively supplanting our own opinions with those of a vanishing generation. The present is not still. It has a forward motion that you must adjust for. Otherwise you will be chronically behind. For in the instant between assessment, decision, and action, the world has not stood still but hurtled forward. Tomorrow is in our hands, quite different than today. The time between is filled with advice for us to critically assess, both old and new. Neither old nor new deserves a free ride.

One must care about a world one will not see.
- Bertrand Russell

If you can look into the seeds of time and say, which grain will grow, and which will not, speak then to me.
- Shakespeare 'Macbeth'

The future comes one day at a time.
- Dean Acheson

The afternoon knows what the morning never suspected.
- Swedish proverb

I never think of the future. It comes soon enough.
- Albert Einstein

Predominant opinions are generally the opinions of the generation that is vanishing.
- Benjamin Disraeli

It is a mistake to look too far ahead. Only one link in the chain of destiny can be handled at a time.
- Winston Churchill

Don't brood on what's past, but never forget it either.
- Thomas H. Raddall

Life can only be understood backward. It must be lived forward.
- Søren Kierkegaard

What's gone and what's past help
should be past grief.

>   -   Shakespeare, 'The Winter's Tale'

Some people are making such thorough preparation for
rainy days that they aren't enjoying today's sunshine.

>   -   William Feather

Skate to where the puck is going and not where it's been.

>   -   Wayne Gretzsky

Tomorrow is the most important thing in life. Comes in
to us at midnight very clean. It's perfect when it arrives
and it puts itself in our hands and hopes we've learnt
something from yesterday.

>   -   John Wayne

Time gives good advice.

>   -   Maltese proverb

There are two kinds of fools: one says, 'This is old,
therefore it is good'; the other says 'This is new, therefore
it is better.'

>   -   Dean William R. Inge

Satisfied / Unsatisfied

Longing takes too long. To pray, to hope, to
dream of someday being satisfied fills too
many every days. What have you seen, or
done or felt today for which you are grateful?
Nothing? Everything? Something? Are your
needs that great compared to others who
somehow find happiness with less? If so the
answer is in the want, not the have. To want
too much in the face of so much need diminishes the wanter, not so much in other's eyes
but in his own. For wanting is insatiable when
it escapes, pulling the wanter along, a victim,
distracted from the life and needs and fulfillment all around. Walk upright and awake to
your surroundings. You have shoes and feet.
Others have neither. If you must want, want to
discover your fullness, and when you arrive,
be that. In the meantime live with what you
have and appreciate it for what it is. Learn to
balance what it is you want with what it is you
have.

Welcome everything that comes to you, but do not long for anything else.

- Andrè Gide

Want is a growing giant whom the coat of Have was never large enough to cover.

- Ralph Waldo Emerson

I murmured because I had no shoes, until I met a man who had no feet.

- Persian Proverb

Learn what you are, and be such.

- Pindar

We must like what we have when we don't have what we like.

- Roger de Bussy-Rabutin

There is a proper balance between not asking enough of oneself and asking or expecting too much.

- May Sarton

Silence / Interruption

Silence is living too. Silence can compete with other forms of living that conspire to crowd it out. Silence makes good friends like peace, and truth, and affection, and careful listening to others. Silence advances strength in spirit and quiet imaginings when not accompanied by loneliness. Growth can occur in silence beyond detection. Silence awakens the senses, allowing you to notice things you never imagined shared your space. These things have shape and size, color and texture, sound and smell, movement and direction. Their little dramas have a story to tell, a relevance to you. Silence allows you to enter their world. Silence is not the same as nothing-ness. Quite the opposite. The reader is silent, yet her mind is full of images and places, thoughts and dreams. In the silence she is transported to other worlds of living that may possess the answers she has sought. That is the point.

Taking time to live is taking time to appreciate simple silence as better than any kind of talk, or watching a flower, or watching a guy wash the windows on a skyscraper and wondering what he is thinking.

- Gersi Douchan

The fair request ought to be followed by the deed, in silence.

- Dante

Go placidly amid the noise and the haste, and remember what peace there may be in silence. As far as possible without surrender, be on good terms with all persons. Speak your truth quietly and clearly, and listen to others, even the dull and the ignorant; they too have their story. Be yourself. Especially do not feign affection. Neither be cynical about love-for in the face of all aridity and disenchantment it is as perennial as the grass. Take kindly the council of the years, gracefully surrendering the things of youth. Nurture strength of spirit to shield you in sudden misfortune. But do not distress yourself with imaginings. Many fears are born of fatigue and loneliness.

- From the works of
Max Ehrmann

Acorns are planted silently by some unnoticed breeze.

- Thomas Carlyle

'Tis the good reader that makes the good book.

- Ralph Waldo Emerson

Certainty / Uncertainty

There are no perfect decisions because there is always room for doubt. Holding steady to a well thought out decision is a sign of maturity. Life is by nature uncertain. That is the fun and the risk in it. Absolute certainty would be the end of growth, the death of possibility. Leaping in the dark uncovers moments of truth. We are never certain until we choose. The choice certifies itself. If you need certainty, be certain that change will never be far removed, and that life has to do with dealing with it. For that's the truth whether we like it or not. In the absence of ironclad assurances, we are still called upon each day to act decisively, to make decisions. It was never intended that we should stand protected, idle and content, for very long. That is not the destiny of the free. Rather we are born to think, to contemplate and to decide. Insecurity comes with the territory.

Soon after a hard decision something inevitably occurs to cast doubt. Holding steady against that doubt usually proves the decision.

-   R. I. Fitzhenry

Maturity is the capacity to endure uncertainty.

-   John Finley

Living is a form of not being sure, not knowing what next, or how. The moment you know how, you begin to die a little. The artist never entirely knows. We guess. We may guess wrong, but we take leap after leap in the dark.

-   Agnes de Mille

We are not certain, we are never certain.

-   Albert Camus

Every area of trouble gives out a ray of hope, and the one unchangeable certainty is that nothing is certain or unchangeable.

-   John F. Kennedy

The central problem of our age is how to act decisively in the absence of certainty.

-   Bertrand Russell

Certainty generally is illusion and repose is not the destiny of man.

-   Oliver Wendell Holmes, Jr.

Free man is by necessity insecure; thinking man is by necessity uncertain.

-   Erich Fromm

Teach / Learn

To teach you must learn twice at least. Once to master the knowledge and once again to refine it as you transfer it to another and incorporate the feedback. Teaching does not automatically assure learning. Not only does the teacher require skill and capability but the learner must be receptive and willing also. Little things can be taught and learnt without much effort from either party. But the larger truths, the principles, processes and values, challenge both sides. They require more than show and tell. They demand immersion. But there is little value in going under water if you do not know or cannot remember to hold your breath. Knowing how to learn should not be pre-sumed. Meaning does not come easily. The fortunate who catch the truth must still mold and shape it to their own reality. To be edu-cable requires openness, an admission of your weakness without the loss of your self-confi-dence. The challenges come as much, if not more, from the other students as from the teacher. Though all are looking forward, the learning occurs sideways. Learners make time to learn knowing it will save time later. Successful teachers teach not from the teachers point of view but from the learners. They realize the younger the student the better the reception, not just because the synapses are superior in number and function but also because there is less to unteach. The best learners want the knowledge badly, need it, and pursue it with deliberate yearning. In the end, both teacher and pupil know the product of success is independence.

To teach is to learn twice.
-      Joseph Joubert

The authority of those who profess to teach is often a positive hindrance to those who desire to learn.
-      Cicero

Whatever is good to know is difficult to learn.
-      Greek proverb

Tell me and I'll forget. Show me, and I may not remember. Involve me, and I'll understand.
-      Native American saying

Experience teaches only the teachable.
-      Aldous Huxley

They know enough who know how to learn.
-      Henry Adams

Each man must look to himself to teach him the meaning of life. It is not something discovered; it is something molded.
-      Antoine de Saint-Exupery

Education is the ability to listen to almost anything without losing your temper or your self-confidence.
-      Robert Frost

I pay the School Master, but 'tis the school boys that educate my son.
-      Ralph Waldo Emerson

It is nonsense to say there is not enough time to be fully informed... Time given to thought is the greatest timesaver of all.

- Norman Cousins

I tried to treat them like me, and some of them weren't.

- Coach Bill Russell, on why he had difficulty with some of his players.

What the mother sings to the cradle goes all the way down to the grave.

- Henry Ward Beecher

Human behavior flows from three main sources: desire, emotion, and knowledge.

- Plato

There are three ingredients in the good life: learning, earning and yearning.

- Christopher Morely

Give a man a fish and you feed him for a day. Teach a man to fish and you feed him for a lifetime.

- Chinese proverb

Superficial / Deep

Shallow foundations are always cause for
worry. They don't support the weight. They
don't resist the storms. They don't accommodate the shifts and strains that come and go
with changes on the ground. People with
foundations, deep livers, fear neither weight,
nor storms, nor shifting ground. They live by
cause and effect, not by luck, more knowledge-
able than well-read. They know who they are
and are content to play that out.

Deep down he is shallow.
-       Political saying

People living deeply have no fear of death.
-       Anaïs Nin

Shallow men believe in luck, wise and strong men in
cause and effect.
-       Ralph Waldo Emerson

Deep versed in books and shallow in himself.
-       John Milton

I think somehow we learn who we really are and then
live with that decision.
-       Eleanor Roosevelt

Replenished — Consumed

What a shame to organize one's life without regard for growth and development, short-sighted, to end premature and used up. What a shame. With planning and good pacing, it is possible to grow reserves. But good and bad expand in equal measure depending on what is exercised. The good grown replenishes. The bad grown consumes. Enthusiasm comes in chasing one's potential. Aspire and achieve and never feel depleted. The competition is with yourself not others. Never to be futile. Never to be hopeless. And if this world does not provide the opportunity to fulfill your every dream, be content to lay the ground for the next generation. Fill it up for them. Much worse than this would be to savage a meager victory and leave behind scorched earth for your children to till. Fame and fortune means little if confined to a single generation. Better for the cup to overflow – not with money, gild or glitter – but with love, and memories and time well-spent generating hope and securing another's future.

A great secret of success is to go through life as a man who never gets used up.
-   Albert Schweitzer

All our talents increase in the using, and every faculty both good and bad strengthens by exercise.
-   Anne Bronte

No one keeps up his enthusiasm automatically. Enthusiasm must be nourished with new actions, new aspirations, new efforts, new vision. Compete with yourself; set your teeth and dive into the job of breaking your own record. It is one's own fault if his enthusiasm is gone; he has failed to feed it.
-   Papyrus

There is no more dreadful punishment than futile and hopeless labor.
-   Albert Camus

I must study politics and war, that my sons may have the liberty to study mathematics and philosophy, geography, natural history, and naval architecture, navigation, commerce, and agriculture, in order to give their children a right to study painting, poetry, music, architecture, statuary, tapestry and porcelain.
-   John Adams

It's not that I'm not grateful for all this attention. It's just that fame and fortune ought to add up to more than fame and fortune.
-   Robert Fulghum

Energized / Bored

Boredom is man's great fear, a succession of ordinary days and ordinary ways. It is common to be bored because idleness is often present and well accepted. Self-sufficiency fills time and benefits twice, once for the effort and once again for the work produced. Self-respect drives most to work. Profit is a pleasant and necessary by-product but not the primary instigator for most. Some appear idle, while deep in thought. They are our creators and their creations become clear with time. To be biased toward a pursuit is a welcome gift which offers pleasure and happiness. If the pursuit is of limited worth, the rewards to the impassioned player remain undeniable. Boredom is costly in productivity lost and as a depressant to society overall. It is the energetic who run the world. It is the fearful who are fatigued. Split your time between work and love and there will be little time left. If there is time left, fill it with walking. It is excellent exercise that is respectful of the body, mindful of the earth below, and well-tolerated by all ages.

A man can stand almost anything except a succession of ordinary days.

> \- Goethe

Of all our faults, the one that we excuse most easily is idleness.

> \- La Rochefoucauld

Chop your own wood and it will warm you twice.

> \- Carved on the cypress wood mantel in Henry Ford's home – Fairlane

Man works primarily for his own self-respect and not for others or for profit…the person who is working for the sake of his own satisfaction, the money he gets in return serves merely as fuel, that is, as a symbol of reward and recognition, in the analysis, of acceptance by one's fellowmen.

> \- Otto Rank

A man is not idle because he is absorbed in thought. There is a visible labour and there is an invisible labour.

> \- Victor Hugo

The high prize of life, the crowning fortune of man, is to be born with a bias to some pursuit which finds him employment and happiness.

> \- Ralph Waldo Emerson

You will do foolish things, but do them with enthusiasm.

> \- Colette

The most costly disease is not cancer or coronaries. The most costly disease is boredom – costly for both individual and society.
- Norman Cousins

The world belongs to the energetic.
- Ralph Waldo Emerson

All forms of fear produce fatigue.
- Bertrand Russell

There is time for work and time for love. That leaves no other time.
- Coco Chanel

Walking is the best possible exercise. Habituate yourself to walk very far.
- Thomas Jefferson

Struggle / Give In

In many ways the human life is defined by
struggle. We should not take life too lightly.
Rather life should be considered dear and rare
and glorious. We measure success by the
obstacles overcome. What you would die for
tells you what you have lived for. Something
just beyond your grasp is worth a struggle.
Adversity strengthens. False admirers do not.
Trouble and handling it are one and the same.
First you learn to struggle, then you learn to
win. Your flower will bloom, but count on
blisters before the job is done. Manage by
understanding that efforts made now are a
down payment for future restful nights. And
giving in to evil forces now only gets you
nightmares later on. Keep eyes wide open.
The greatest challenges are well hidden, or in
areas where you lack either aptitude or interest
or both, or in areas where your great passion is
shared by no one, at least at first. With all of
these obstacles to overcome, how do strugglers
succeed? They don't give up. They don't
pretend. And life goes on.

The harder the conflict, the more glorious the triumph. What we obtain too cheap, we esteem too lightly; 'tis dearness only that gives everything it's value.

- Thomas Paine

Success is to be measured not so much by the position that one has reached in life as by the obstacles he has overcome trying to succeed.

- Booker T. Washington

If a man hasn't discovered something that he will die for, he isn't fit to live.

- Martin Luther King

Ah, but man's reach should exceed his grasp, or what's a heaven for?

- Robert Browning

(Adversity is) the state in which a man most easily becomes acquainted with himself, being especially free from admirers then.

- Samuel Johnson

If I had a formula for bypassing trouble, I wouldn't pass it around. Wouldn't be doing anybody a favor. Trouble creates a capacity to handle it. I don't say I embrace trouble. That's as bad as treating it as an enemy. But I do say, meet it as a friend, for you'll see a lot of it and had better be on speaking terms with it.

- Oliver Wendell Holms, Jr.

The nature of the flower is to bloom.

- Alice Walker

If you want a place in the sun, you've got to put up with a few blisters.

- Abigail van Buren

When you can't solve the problem, manage it.
- Robert H. Schuller

Every difficulty slurred over will be a ghost to disturb your repose later on.
- Frederic Chopin

No man can become really educated without having pursued some study in which he took no interest. For it is part of education to interest ourselves in subjects for which we have no aptitude.
- T. S. Eliot

One may have a blazing hearth in one's soul, and yet no one ever comes to sit by it.
- Vincent van Gogh

Actively we have woven ourselves with the very warp and woof of this nation, — we have fought their battles, shared their sorrow, mingled our blood with theirs, and generation after generation have pleaded with a head-strong, careless people to despise not Justice, Mercy, and Truth, lest the nation be smitten with a curse. Our song, our toil, our cheer, and warning have been given to this nation in blood-brotherhood. Are not these gifts worth the giving? Is not this work and striving? Would America have been American without her Negro people?
- W.E.B. DuBois

In three words I can sum up everything I have learned about life. It goes on.

- Robert Frost

The crisis you have to worry about most is the one you don't see coming.

- Mike Mansfield

Praise/Criticism

Criticism practiced well is counsel, practiced poorly, a disincentive. Praise practiced well is motivational, practiced poorly enabling. To be complimented, especially with good timing and when deserved, can be a source of strength and energy, and remembered for a lifetime. The same is true of criticism especially if unjust, or public, or written down to be preserved on paper. Gossip is criticism with no discipline and little purpose but to entertain. There is no scarcity of criticism on this earth. If you desire to escape it completely, you will have to resign from this world – nothing to do, nothing to say, nothing to be. If every one admires you perhaps you follow too much. Try leading. Try modeling. It will lead you to true friends, and occasionally a foe.

It is well enough, when one is talking to a friend, to lodge in an odd word by way of council now and then; but there is something mighty irksome in its staring upon one in a letter, where one ought to see only kind words and friendly remembrances.
- Mary Lamb

I can live for two months on a good complement.
- Mark Twain

No one gossips about other people's secret virtues.
- Bertrand Russell

Danger and delight grow on one stalk.
- Old saying

To escape criticism – do nothing, say nothing, be nothing.
- Elbert Hubbard

Woe unto you, when all men shall speak well of you.
- Luke 6:26

Those things that hurt, instruct.
- Benjamin Franklin

Children have more need of models than of critics.
- Joseph Joubert

He makes no friends who never made a foe.
- Alfred, Lord Tennyson

Faith-Filled / Cynical

Fidelity, commitment to a worthy purpose. Given little else, this is enough for happiness. Keeping the faith. Fighting the fight. Taking a risk to benefit someone other than yourself, with God on your side, at your side. Faith is to believe in an attainable future, to believe in yourself, and to believe in a connection between the two. A single spirit can ignite a brilliant flame, and light the way toward change. That extra light's a help because, with each step, certainty can never be assured. Risk is always there even for the explorer. Faith is an inner strength, exposed by trial. It is invincible but absent in those consumed by fear. Fear and doubt are a powerless couple, and prophesize their own defeat, rushing headlong to their own doom. Faith takes time, gives time, and is of positive assistance to those who will try. Faith is flow, the ability to be drawn along by the current without need to resist or control one's every movement or destiny, without need to quarrel with the world.

Many persons have a wrong idea of what constitutes true happiness. It is not attained through self-gratification, but through fidelity to a worthy purpose.

- Helen Keller

I have fought a good fight, I have finished my course, I have kept the faith.

- 2 Timothy 4:7

Without risk, faith is an impossibility.

- Søren Kierkegaard

God will be present, whether asked or not.

- Latin proverb

Now faith is the substance of things hoped for, the evidence of things not seen.

- Hebrews 11:1

There is not enough darkness in all the world to put out the light of even one small candle.

- Robert Alden

Every human being is born without faith. Faith comes only through the process of making decisions to change before we can be sure it's the right move.

- Robert H. Schuller

In the depth of winter, I finally learned that there was in me an invincible summer.

- Albert Camus

Fear is the absence of faith.

- Paul Tillich

Doubt is a pain too lonely to know that faith is his twin brother.

- Kahlil Gibran

If you keep on saying things are going to be bad, you have a good chance of being a prophet.

- Isaac Bashevis Singer

Give God time.

- The Koran

Faith moves mountains, but you have to keep pushing while you are praying.

- Mason Cooley

As your faith is strengthened, you will find that there is no longer the need to have a sense of control, that things will flow as they will, and that you will flow with them, to your great delight and benefit.

- Emmanuel

I had a lover's quarrel with the world.

- Robert Frost

Character / Reputation

Character building is a lifelong pursuit, the creation of self in pursuit of your full potential. It is effected by those who bear us and reinforced by how they raise us. Its formation should be judged within the context of our times and the events surrounding us. Storms create and reflect our character. Character is about our finer features, those that will be remembered for all time. Reputations, in contrast, come and go and are the work of other persons, opinions that will vary with the winds. Take care then in adjustments made to win the favor of others. Such compromises made may enhance your reputation by sending your character into decline. And avoid doing things you would be embarrassed for others to know you did. Wish only to be who you are. That is enough if you live it fully. Character does not rely on success. It is more fundamental, preceding and outlasting all rewards. It is what your name stands for, and when lost is hard to recover. Keep your head about you. Trust yourself. Be patient. Avoid lies and hatred. Dream but not too much. Think but not all the time. Embrace good times and bad without overreacting to either. Take risks when they are called for. Stand out in a crowd without looking down on others. Don't be afraid to touch. Be firm in your convictions. Do what's right. Know what's right. Believe in others but do not bend to others who threaten or bully. See the earth. Walk the earth. Be yourself.

Character building begins in our infancy, and continues until death.
- Eleanor Roosevelt

It is always wise, as it is also fair, to test a man by the standards of his own day, and not by those of another
- Odell Shepard

Talents are best nurtured in solitude: character is best formed in the stormy billows of the world.
- Goethe

Character is what God and the angels know of us; reputation is what men and women think of us.
- Horace Mann

If I trim myself to suit others I will soon whittle myself away.
- Anon.

If you don't want anyone to know it, don't do it.
- Chinese proverb

Do not wish to be anything but what you are, and try to be that perfectly.
- St. Francis de Sales

Character is that which can do without success.
- Ralph Waldo Emerson

Have regard for your name, since it will remain for you longer than a great store of gold.
- Ecclesiasticus 42:12

If you can keep your head when all about you
Are losing theirs and blaming it on you:
If you can trust yourself when all men doubt you,
But make allowance for their doubting too;
If you can wait and not be tired of waiting,
Or being lied about, don't deal in lies,
Or being hated, don't give way to hatred

And yet don't look too good nor talk too wise;
If you can dream – and not make dreams your master;
If you can think, and not make thoughts your aim,
If you can meet with Triumph and Disaster,
And treat those two imposters just the same,

If you can make one heap of all your winnings
And risk it on one turn of pitch-and-toss,
And lose, and start again at your beginnings
And never breathe a word about your loss…
If you can talk with crowds and keep your virtue,
Or walk with Kings nor lose the common touch,
If neither foes nor loving friends can hurt you,
If all men count with you, but none too much;
If you can fill the unforgiving minute
With sixty seconds' worth of distance run,
Yours is the Earth and everything that's in it,
And – which is more – you'll be a Man my son!

-     Rudyard Kipling

Experienced / Inexperienced

To what do we owe experience? Mostly time.
Sometimes place or privilege. Recording life is
not the same as living life, but merely a damp-
ened down safe substitute. Experience can be,
often is painful. Count on a few scars. It's a
rocky road to maturity, with courage rising
with each step. Standing still bequeaths no
strength. Momentum is required. No one gets
there overnight. Experience is skills and learning built on other skills and learnings. First
walk, then fly. Experience is not a list of happenings but rather the effect of the happenings
on one human life. While there may be nothing new, to you, it's new. And each time the
learning must be extracted. Just because someone else walked the road doesn't mean she
walked it for you. Take your own path, not in
dreams but in the flesh. Grow into yourself
and then grow out of yourself. Begin a taker
and become a giver.

Everything happens to everybody sooner or later if there is time enough.
- George Bernard Shaw

How vain it is to sit down to write when you have not stood up to live.
- Henry David Thoreau

God will not look you over for medals, degrees or diplomas, but for scars!
- Elbert Hubbard

How many roads must a man walk down
Before you call him a man?
- Bob Dylan

A great part of courage is the courage of having done the thing before.
- Ralph Waldo Emerson

He who would learn to fly one day must first learn to stand and walk and run and climb and dance; one cannot fly into flying.
- Friedrich Nietzsche

Experience is not what happens to a man. It is what a man does with what happens to him.
- Aldous Huxley

There is nothing new under the sun.
- Ecclesiastes 1:9

Imagination is a poor substitute for experience.
- Havelock Ellis

Genius / Talent

Talent is a wonderful thing especially when it's
shared. Out of the sharing comes improve-
ments in the human condition, a sense of
empowerment with the knowledge that we do
have the resources to address life's challenges,
and an expansion of the overall talent pool
since talent is transferable. Talent is about
getting the job done. It is a reflection of capacity and capability. You do because you can, not
because it is your calling. In this sense talent is
bottom up, not top down. People grow talents,
never too proud to tap the brains of others.
But genius comes at the world in a different
way with passion, commitment and belief that
a single thought, your own, holds true for
other men, if not today then with tomorrow's
arrival. It is a preparing of the world that
would generally rather be left alone. Thinkers
and their thoughts are so destabilizing that
they routinely instigate organized opposition,
segregating and then pairing visionary and
repressive powers in an uncomfortable duet.
Those in the status quo say, in retrospect, given
the data we gave him, anyone would know
what he predicted. But there is no sufficient

explanation for the fact that he, the genius did, and they did not, given the same world, the same reality from which to derive the truth. And furthermore, the genius saw the big picture in a larger way and the smaller picture in a more simple form all at once. There is after all a difference between creating the concept and having the talent to execute it. Many have the latter while few possess the former.

Talent is always conscious of its own abundance, and does not object to sharing.
- Aleksander Solzhenitsyn

Genius does what it must, and talent does what it can.
- Edward Bulwer- Lytton

I hate intellectuals. They are from the top down. I am from the bottom up.
- Frank Lloyd Wright

I not only use all the brains I have, but all I can borrow.
- Woodrow Wilson

To believe your own thought, to believe that what is true for you in your private heart is true for all men – that is genius.
- Ralph Waldo Emerson

When true genius appears in the world you may know him by this sign, that the dunces are all in confederacy against him.
- Jonathan Swift

Too often we forget that genius...depends on the data within its reach, that Archimedes could not have devised Edison's inventions.
- Ernest Dimnet

Any intelligent fool can make things bigger, more complex, and more violent. It takes a touch of genius – and a lot of courage – to move in the opposite direction.
- E.F. Schumacher

223

Wish (For It) / Go (For It)

Desires unfulfilled breed strong emotions.
Some ask God for help before they ask themselves. It takes courage and backbone to pursue a dream. Standing around and wishing
doesn't get the job done. It simply creates
delay and discontent in you and others. It's up
to you. Seeking's not enough. You must find.
When you find it, keep it in view and pursue it.
Never look back or second guess your first best
guess. After all, a guess is all it is. And if
you're wrong, at least you tried. Stars that you
pursue are more than a destination. They shed
light. If you'll commit, then so will others, in
view and out of view. The world is full of
helpers but first you need a doer to ignite. Go
with what you've got. If you have to do it, it is
likely you'll succeed. Far better to have tried
than ever hear your lips repeat "I could have, I
should have."

He who desires, but acts not, breeds pestilence.
-     William Blake

Ask God's blessing on your work, but don't ask him to
do it for you.
-     Dame Flora Robson

Never grow a wishbone, daughter, where your backbone
ought to be.
-     Clementine Paddleford

This one makes a net, this one stands and wishes.
Would you like to make a bet which one gets the fishes?
-     Chinese Rhyme

If it is to be
It is up to me.

-     William H. Johnson

I do not seek. I find.
-     Pablo Picasso

I can tell you how to get what you want: You've just got
to keep a thing in view and go for it and never let your
eyes wander to right or left or up or down. And looking
back is fatal.
-     William J. Lock

He turns not back who is bound to a star.
-     Leonardo da Vinci

The moment one definitely commits oneself, then Providence moves too. All sorts of things occur to help that would never otherwise have occurred. A stream of events issues from the decision, raising unforeseen incidents and meetings and material assistance, which no man could have dreamt would have come his way.

    -    W. H. Murray

Let us act on what we have, since we have not what we wish.

    -    Cardinal Newman

What one has to do usually can be done.

    -    Eleanor Roosevelt

Of all sad words of tongue or pen, the saddest are these: It might have been.

    -    John Greenleaf Whittier

Knowledge / Ignorance

To be prejudiced is the most fundamental form
of ignorance expressed. The bigotry itself is so
deeply flawed that it is easily disproved by
observation and the expression of children.
Great realms of information collected in defense do not change the facts. Foolish is foolish! We know what we know and the opposite
as well. The key to breaking through is to
understand each other and the facts. This
requires effort, time, energy and persistence.
But failure to commit these resources is far
more expensive. Investment in knowledge is
always well spent and represents a permanent
gain that cannot be taken away. There is always room for knowledge, for each of us
harbors ignorance of some sort which knowledge could displace. Always be at peace with
the words "I do not know." Holding fast to
ignorance is proof of stupidity, while embracing and acknowledging ignorance opens one to
the joys of learning. Mistakes along the way
punctuate growth. Repeating the same mistake renders no additional value. And jump-
ing from the narrow experience of one discreet
event to broad confidence in a general truth is

too big a jump too soon. Learning is asleep inside each of us waiting to be stirred. Judgment, not statistics, is what we seek because important questions are more susceptible to qualitative answers. We all want to know. For this we write books, to remember, to reflect, to relearn.

Prejudice is the child of ignorance.
- William Hazlett

The mind of a bigot is like the pupil of the eye; the more light you pour upon it, the more it will contract.
- Oliver Wendell Holmes, Jr.

We're drowning in information and starving for knowledge.
- Rutherford D. Rogers

If fifty million people say a foolish thing, it is still a foolish thing.
- Anatole France

To know that we know what we know, and that we do not know what we do not know, that is true knowledge.
- Henry David Thoreau

Everyone hears only what he understands.
- Goethe

If you think education is expensive – try ignorance.
- Derek Bok

If a man empties his purse into his head, no one can take it from him.
- Benjamin Franklin

Everybody is ignorant, only on different subjects.
- Will Rogers

Obstinacy and heat in sticking to one's opinions is the surest proof of stupidity. Is there anything so cock-sure, so immovable, so disdainful, so contemplative, so solemn and serious as an ass?
-    Michel de Montaigne

One of the greatest joys known to man is to take flight into ignorance in search of knowledge.
-    Robert Lynd

Any man can make mistakes, but only an idiot persists in his error.
-    Cicero

No man can reveal to you aught but that which already lies half asleep in the dawning of your knowledge.
-    Kahlil Gibran

Statistics are no substitute for judgment.
-    Henry Clay

Almost all important questions are important precisely because they are not susceptible to quantitative answer.
-    Arthur Schlesinger, Jr.

All men by nature desire to know.
-    Aristotle

All the glory of the world would be buried in oblivion, unless God had provided mortals with the remedy of books.
-    Richard De Bury

Bold / Cautious

Daring to fail is a sign of greatness. To be challenged and in the center of controversy, to persist, is a measure of the person. Being on guard is all defense, watch and wait, watch and wait, while others take the offense, others run the gauntlet. The bold try something new for the very first time. If it tastes badly, they spit it out, and try another plate. Life is after all experience. The timid rarely reap rewards, nor should they having taken zero risk. Fortune does favor the bold. The bold take action in words as well as deeds. They say what others think, disrupting, disturbing, not out of harm or by intention but by simply telling the truth. They deserve neither disgrace nor separation from the whole. Rather they have earned a higher elevation for tearing off the cloth that hid the truth, for moving others down the path of needed change. The cautious wait in quiet to be assigned a task. The bold are always busy. The opportunities for leadership are piled high for lack of competition.

Only those who dare to fail greatly can ever achieve greatly.
- Robert F. Kennedy

The ultimate measure of a man is not where he stands in moments of comfort and convenience, but where he stands at times of challenge and controversy.
- Martin Luther King, Jr.

You don't learn to hold your own in the world by standing on guard, but by attacking, and getting well hammered yourself.
- George Bernard Shaw

He was a bold man that first ate an oyster.
- Jonathan Swift

Do not be too timid and squeamish about your actions. All life is an experience.
- Ralph Waldo Emerson

Fortune favours the bold.
- Virgil

To know how to say what others only know how to think is what makes men poets or sages; and to dare to say what others only dare to think makes men martyrs or reformers or both.
- Elizabeth Charles

No great man ever complains of want of opportunity.
- Ralph Waldo Emerson

Young/Old

Old or young is not an either/or but a continuum of growth. Babies start so nice, its
undeniable. But they have a lot to learn. Maturity arrives on the other end but with a price,
a prejudice toward caution which can be a
positive hindrance to tackling the impossible –
and succeeding. The years pass in a space of
time, but each time's different, so no two lives
are the same. Some would reverse the order,
begin at 80 and move the other way. But even
if we could, would we ever arrive at 18 going
that way? Each age has its way. What seems
good to me now seemed boring to me then.
Back then I knew the rules, now I know how to
break them. Certain things like hope and
kindness and good cheer do not smooth out
the wrinkles but can keep the heart refreshed.
And honored age does carry with it the authority to ignore authority. You learn to forego
your age or at least not to dwell on it, to be
happy just to be alive, to have that privilege. If
not years to your life, why not life to your
years? To grow old with a best friend and have
time contained in joined hands, how great is
that? Great enough to not fear having to say

goodbye or daring to tell the truth? I'd say yes
if only to enjoy the ride. And when the time
comes, whether in a storm or calm, let down
the sails and join quietly the waves.

Anyone who stops learning is old, whether at twenty or eighty. Anyone who keeps learning stays young. The greatest thing in life is to keep your mind young.

- Henry Ford

Babies are such a nice way to start people.

- Don Herold

Age is a high price to pay for maturity.

- Tom Stoppard

The young do not know enough to be prudent, and therefore they attempt the impossible – and achieve it, generation after generation.

- Pearl S. Buck

Don't limit a child to your own learning, for he was born in another time.

- Rabbinical saying

Life would be infinitely happier if we could only be born at the age of eighty and gradually approach eighteen.

- Mark Twain

In the last few years everything I'd done up to sixty or so has seemed very childish.

- T. S. Eliot

It is not the years in your life but the life in your years that counts.

- Adlai Stevenson

To keep the heart unwrinkled, to be hopeful, kindly, cheerful, reverent – that is to triumph over old age.

- Thomas Bailey Aldrich

Old age, especially an honored old age, has so great authority, that this is of more value than all the pleasures of youth.

-    Cicero

How old would you be if you didn't know how old you are?

-    Satchel Paige

I'm very pleased with each advancing year. It stems back to when I was forty. I was a bit upset about reaching that milestone, but an older friend consoled me. 'Don't complain about growing old – many people don't have that privilege.'

-    Earl Warren

Grow old with me!
The best is yet to be,
The last of life, for which the first was made:
Our times are in his hands
Who sayeth "a whole I plant,
Youth shows but half;
Trust God; see all nor be afraid."

-    Robert Browning

I speak the truth, not so much as I would, but as much as I dare; and I dare a little more, as I grow older.

-    Michel de Montaigne

It is time to be old,
To take in sail.

-    Ralph Waldo Emerson

Rejoice / Sorrow

Sorrow is a special form of vulnerability, temporarily rendering a person childlike without defense. It is isolating, but less so as we learn how common is this experience shared. Nature teaches loss and recovery, suffering survived. How good to be alive. Lose a little, learn a lot – that's the way upward. Joy will come for those willing to wait. For we were not born to get through free of pain. The things for which there is no control, what choice is left but acceptance? Luckily for us, the human spirit is remarkably sturdy and resilient, allowing most hardship to be bearable as long as we can tell the little from the big and find a way to smile through.

Sorrow makes us all children again.
- Ralph Waldo Emerson

In extreme youth, in our most humiliating sorrow, we think we are alone. When we are older we find that others have suffered too.
- Suzanne Moarny

Birds sing after a storm; why shouldn't people feel as free to delight in whatever remains to them?
- Rose Fitzgerald Kennedy

To lose
Is to learn.
- Anon.

Weeping may endure for a night, but joy cometh in the morning.
- Psalms

Every man shall bear his own burden.
- Galatians 6:5

Be willing to have it so; acceptance of what has happened is the first step to overcoming the consequences of any misfortune.
- William James

Life is made up of sobs, sniffles, and smiles, with sniffles predominating.
- O. Henry

Life / Death

Death is not popular but it is inevitable. The
only question is whether it is part of a continuum or something stolen away in the night.
Death is not our choice in time or place. But
life can be lived with death included. Those
who never contribute never live fully. Their
lives are like a series of small deaths, death to
potential, death to promise, death to exploration. Life deserves to be lived each day, considering the unpredictability of death. Life is a
continuum – being, doing, doing without.
Things wear out. They break or get broken by
events beyond our understanding. Life is
short. But the art of living is long. When we
change, there is a sadness for what we leave
behind, but a joy as well for what lies ahead.
It's a trade-off. Losing a love along the way,
that is the pain, depopulation, a hole in your
world. Can it ever be filled? Perhaps not, but
is that not a tribute to the one who's gone, to
the memory of the one whose pleasures made?
No time to fret. No need to rush it. Death will
stop for you so why watch out, or dwell on it.
A better rest, and well-deserved, a joining
'wither thou goest' are in your future too.

You don't get to choose how you're going to die. Or when.
You can only decide how you're going to live. Now.
- Joan Baez

When you cease to make a contribution, you begin to die.
- Eleanor Roosevelt

Learn as if you were going to live forever. Live as if you
were going to die tomorrow.
- Anon.

Fear not that thy life shall come to an end, but rather that it
shall never have a beginning.
- John Henry Cardinal Newman

The great business of life is to be, to do, to do without and
depart.
- John Morley

Everything passes; everything wears out; everything
breaks. (Tout passé, tout lasse, tout casse.)
- French proverb

Art is long, life is short. (Ars longa, vita brevis.)
- Hippocrates

All changes, even the most longed for, have their
melancholy, for what we leave behind us is a part of
ourselves; we must die to one life before we can enter into
another.
- Anatole France

Sometimes, when one person is missing, the whole world seems depopulated.
- Alphonse de Lamartine

Where you used to be, there is a hole in the world, which I find myself constantly walking around in the daytime, and falling into at night. I miss you like hell.
- Edna St. Vincent Millay

The test of pleasure is the memory it leaves behind. (die Probe Eines Genusses ist Sein Errinnerung.)
- Jean Paul Richter

Because I could not stop for Death
He kindly stopped for me –
The carriage held but just ourselves
And Immortality.
- Emily Dickinson

It is a far, far better thing that I do, than anything I have ever done; it is a far, far, better rest that I go to, than I have ever known.
- Charles Dickens

Entreat me not to leave thee, or to return from following after thee; for whither thou goest, I will go; and where thou lodgest, I will lodge; thy people shall be my people and thy God my God: where thou diest will I die, and there will I be buried; the Lord do so to me, and more also, if aught but death part thee and me.
- Ruth 1:16-17

Index of Biographies

Acheson, Dean (1893–1971). U.S. Secretary of State. As Undersecretary of State from 1945 to 1947, Acheson helped develop the Marshall Plan, the Truman Doctrine, and America's policy towards the Soviet Union. As Secretary of State from 1947 to 1953 he helped to create NATO and to rebuild Germany. He advised Presidents Kennedy and Johnson and recommended withdrawal from Vietnam. The author of numerous books on politics, his 1969 memoirs, *Present at the Creation*, received a Pulitzer Prize.

Adams, Henry (1838-1918). American writer and historian. Adams taught history at Harvard and edited the *North American Review*. He wrote novels, essays on the philosophy of history, and historical studies. His most widely read book is *The Education of Henry Adams*. Beautifully written, it uses the story of Adams' intellectual development to explore the civilization of his time.

Adams, John (1735-1826). United States president. Born in Braintree, Massachusetts, Adams was an able lawyer, noted for his honesty and learning. In 1765 his opposition to the Stamp Act, a British tax, made him known throughout the colonies. Once the American Revolution had begun, Adams was among the first to propose American independence. He helped to draft the Declaration of Independence and to persuade its adoption by the Second Continental Congress. He served as a diplomat in Europe, and then as George Washington's vice president. In 1796 he became the second president of the United States. An important American political philosopher, Adams wrote *A Defense of the Constitutions of Governments of the United States of America* and *Discourses on Davila*.

Addison, Joseph (1672–1719). English writer and statesman. Addison, a distinguished classical scholar at Oxford was commissioned by the government to write a poem commemorating a 1704 British military victory. The popularity of the poem, "The Campaign", made Addison's literary reputation and resulted in his appointment as Undersecretary of State. Addison had a long political career, and was considered an important author in his time. The works for which he is most remembered today are his graceful, precise, well-ordered essays, written for publications such as the *Tatler* and the *Spectator*.

Aeschylus (525–456 B.C.). Athenian tragic dramatist. Aeschylus fought at Marathon and at Salamis. In 476 B.C. he went to Sicily to live at the court of Hiero I. He wrote about ninety plays. Seven complete works survive. Aeschylus' tragedies introduced innovations such as costumes and stage decoration, and the presence of more than one actor, which allowed for dramatic conflict. In his tragedies, transgressions are punished, and people learn from their suffering, so that suffering has moral significance. Aeschylus' vivid characters, complex themes, and captivating lyricism make his tragedies some of the greatest ever written.

Alcott, Louisa May (1832-88). American writer. Born in Germantown, Pennsylvania, Louisa May Alcott was the daughter a leading transcendentalist and educational reformer. She served as a nurse during the Civil War, and worked as a servant and a seamstress to supplement her family's meager income before her children's book *Little Women* brought her fame and fortune. The loving, idealistic March family in *Little Women* were modeled on the Alcott family; headstrong Jo March was modeled after Alcott herself. Alcott wrote many other novels for young readers, all offering a warm and lively portrait of family life, as well as two novels for adults.

Alden, Robert (1937-). American clergyman. Born in Massachussets, Alden, a Baptist minister, has been a professor at Conservative Baptist Theological Seminary since 1966. He is the author of several books on the Bible.

Aldrich, Thomas Bailey (1836-1907). American writer. Born in Portsmouth, New Hampshire, Aldrich left school at 13 to work as a clerk in New York City. He soon began writing for periodicals, becoming a literary critic and eventually editor of *The Atlantic Monthly*. His short stories and poems often drew on the New England culture of his youth.

Ali, Muhammad (1942-). American boxer. Born Cassius Clay in Louisville, Kentucky, Ali began boxing at age 12. At age 22, he beat Sonny Liston , becoming heavyweight champion of the world. Ali attracted attention not just for his strength, speed and grace in the ring but for his witty, rhyming boasts. Early on in his professional career, Ali became politically active. His outspoken stance against racial injustice, as well as his conversion to the Nation of Islam, won him many enemies, as did his stance as a conscientious objector in Vietnam. When he refused induction into the armed services in 1967, he was stripped of his title and banned from boxing. His conviction for violating the draft laws was eventually overturned, and he returned to boxing in 1971. He retired in 1981, and was the only man to win the heavyweight championship three times. Ali is renowned around the world, not only as a boxer, but as a man who was willing to sacrifice fame and fortune to stand up for his principles.

Allen, Woody (1935-). American filmmaker and comedian. Allen became a popular stand-up comedian in the 1960s. He soon began writing, directing, and acting in films. His humor draws on his middle-class Brooklyn Jewish background and his neurotic, self-deprecating persona. Allen's films have become increasingly complex over the years, evolving from capers such as 1973's *Sleeper* to films such as 1977's *Annie Hall*, which blend Allen's absurdist humor with serious themes.

Amiel, Henri Frédéric (1821–81). Swiss writer and philosopher. Amiel was a professor of moral philosophy and aesthetics in Geneva. He became known after his death, with the publication of his introspective diary, *Journal Intime*.

Arbus, Diane (1923-71). American photographer. Born in New York City, Arbus studied with Lisette Model, whose influence can be seen in her strange, unsettling portraits. In the early 1960's Arbus worked on freelance projects for *The New York Times Magazine, Harper's Bazaar*, and other magazines. Arbus' photographs show a sometimes "freakish", always mysterious side of her sitters and of American life. Since her suicide in 1971, her art has often received a darker, more autobiographical interpretation. Arbus remains one of the most influential American photographers.

Aristotle (384–322 B.C.). Greek philosopher. Aristotle studied under Plato at the Academy, where he wrote many eloquent dialogues. He later tutored Alexander the Great at the Macedonian court. When he returned to Athens he opened a school in the Lyceum. Aristotle's extant writings include *Physics, Metaphysics, De Anima, Ethics, De Poetica* and *Rhetoric*. Aristotle considered philosophy to be the discerning of the first principles that form the basis of all knowledge. He introduced new concepts in logic and in causality. Following Plato, he argued that the virtue of a thing lay in the realization of its specific nature. For humans, this nature is rationality. In science, Aristotle believed that theory must follow fact, and emphasized observation from nature. Aristotle has had a key role in shaping Western thought.

Armstrong, Neil (1930-). American astronaut. Born in Wapakoneta, Ohio, Armstrong was a fighter pilot during the Korean War, and later a test pilot. He became an astronaut in 1962, and was command pilot of the Gemini 8 mission. His 1969 moonwalk, as commander of Apollo 11, was a powerful moment in the history of humankind's quest for knowledge.

Augustine, Saint (354-430). Born in Tagaste, a Roman town in Northern Africa, Augustine was brought up a Christian by his mother, St. Monica. He was sent to study in Carthage, where he joined the Manicheans, a Christian sect. A skilled rhetorician, he went to Rome and Milan to teach. In Milan, he underwent the crisis that in his *Confessions* figures as the turning point in his life. Influenced by neoplatonism and the teachings of St. Ambrose, Augustine wrestled spiritually and intellectually with sin, faith, and redemption. After two years of inner turmoil, Augustine had himself baptized and became a monk. He later became a priest and a bishop. St. Augustine's writings have had a tremendous impact on the development of Christianity.

Aung San Suu Kui (1945–). Burmese political leader. Aung San Suu Kui is the daughter of assassinated nationalist General Aung San, whose resistance to British colonial rule culminated in Burma's independence in 1948. Aung Sun Suu Kui moved to England to attend university, where she married and had two children . Upon returning to Burma in 1988 she joined the opposition to Burma's brutal military regime and became leader of the National League for Democracy (NLD). Inspired by the non-violent campaigns of Martin Luther King and Gandhi, Aung San Suu Kui traveled around Burma organizing rallies and calling for peaceful democratic reforms and free elections. Her popularity as a leader and, because of her father, as a symbol, to the pro-democracy movement led the government to place her under house arrest in 1989. The NLD won 80% of the seats in 1990 elections for parliament, but the military refused to yield power. Awarded the 1991 Nobel Peace Prize, she remained under house arrest until 1995 and has since been subject to severe restrictions. She has stayed in Burma, continuing to work for her cause. In September 2000, she was again placed under house arrest.

Bacon, Francis (1561–1626). English philosopher, essayist, and statesman. Born in London, Bacon became a member of Parliament in 1584, and an advisor to Queen Elizabeth. During the reign of James I, Bacon advanced politically until 1621, when he was accused of taking bribes as Lord Chancellor. He confessed, and though he was pardoned, his career was over. In retirement, Bacon concentrated exclusively on his writings. His philosophical work *Novum Organum*, which stressed observation and experimentation, was a major contribution to the scientific method. His *Essays* are his most literary and best-known works.

Baez, Joan (1941-). American folksinger. Born in Staten Island, New York, Baez left Boston University to sing in Boston coffee houses. She gave memorable performances at the Newport Folk Festival in 1959 and 1960, and became a popular singer in the 1960s revival of traditional folk music. A leading voice of her activist generation, Baez also sang protest songs and gave concerts in support of civil rights, human rights and the anti-war movement.

Bailey, P.J. (1816-1902). English poet. Philip James Bailey was the author of *Festus*, based on the Faust myth, and *The Universal World*.

Baldwin, James (1924-87). American writer. Born in New York City's Harlem, Baldwin grew up poor. At age 14 he became a Pentecostal preacher, an experience he drew on for his 1953 novel *Go Tell It on the Mountain*. At age 17, Baldwin forsook religion, and moved to the free-thinking, artistic neighborhood of Greenwich Village. He supported himself with odd jobs, and began writing short stories and essays. Some of these were included in his 1955 collection *Notes of a Native Son*. In 1948, Baldwin, tired of the prejudice he faced in America as a black person and a homosexual, moved to Paris. There he wrote his first novels. He returned in 1957 to participate in the civil rights movement. His essay collection *The Fire Next Time* brought Baldwin prominence as an eloquent and passionate voice for racial justice. Baldwin eventually returned to Paris, where he lived for the rest of his life.

Baldwin, Stanley (1867-1947). English statesman. The son of an industrialist, Baldwin spent his early years managing his father's iron, steel, and railway concerns. From 1908 to 1937 he was a member of the House of Commons. He was prime minister three times between 1923 and 1937. His failure to formulate a decisive foreign policy in the face of Hitler's aggression has been widely criticized.

Ballou, Hosea (1771-1852). American Universalist clergyman. Born in Cumberland, Rhode Island, Ballou was ordained a minister of the Universalist Church in 1794. He was important in spreading the Universalist belief that God will ultimately save all mankind. The founder and editor of two Universalist periodicals, Ballou's many writings include pamphlets, poems, hymns, letters, and approximately 10,000 sermons.

Bankhead, Tallulah (1902-68). American actress. Born in Huntsville, Alabama, Bankhead was the daughter of a U.S. congressman. As a child, despite a strict convent education, she was outspoken and made herself the center of attention. After winning a local beauty contest, she landed small roles in silent films, and in 1918 made her Broadway debut. She quickly became a star, known as much for her spectacularly outrageous behavior as for her acting. Her work in movies was disappointing, but she gave brilliant performances in plays such as the 1939 production of *The Little Foxes.*

Barnes, Djuna (1892–1982). American author. Born in Cornwall, New York, Barnes studied art in New York City, illustrated, and wrote short stories, poetry, and plays. She lived in Paris from 1920 to 1940, then returned to New York City where she lived in near isolation for the rest of her life. Her best-known work is her 1936 modernist novel *Nightwood.*

Basil, Saint (c.330-379). Greek bishop. After being converted to a religious life by his sister, St. Macrina, Basil spent some time in religious retreat. He wrote rules upon which the life of Basilian monks is based. He became head of most of the church in Asia Minor, and helped define orthodoxy. He is one of the four fathers of the Greek Church.

Beard, Charles A. (1874–1948). American historian. Born near Knightstown, Indiana, Beard became a professor of politics at Columbia University in 1907. He advocated incorporating the study of economics, politics, intellectual life, and all aspects of culture into the teaching of history. After resigning from Columbia in World War I, he helped to found the New School for Social Research, and was director of the Training School for Public Service in New York City. Much of Beard's work examines the economic basis of politics. Beard became known to the general public through *The Rise of American Civilization* and its sequels, which he wrote in collaboration with his wife, historian Mary Ritter Beard.

Beecher, Henry Ward (1813-1887). American preacher. Beecher was pastor of the Plymouth Church in Brooklyn, New York from 1847 until his death. From his pulpit, he addressed every important issue of his time. A brilliant speaker, Beecher attracted huge audiences. He also edited two periodicals dedicated to religion and politics. Beecher was an abolitionist leader and a proponent of women's rights, particularly suffrage.

Behan, Brendan (1923–64). Irish author. Born in Dublin, Behan grew up in poverty. He owed much of his education to his family, which was well-read and had strong Republican sympathies. Behan joined the Irish Repulbican Army in 1937, and spent time in prison for political offences. Behan's lively, humorous plays and stories colorfully depict the life of ordinary working people. His work includes the grimly comic 1956 drama *The Quare Fellow* and 1962's *Brendan Behan's Island: an Irish Sketch-Book* .

Benny, Jack (1894-1974). American comedian. Born Benjamin Kubelsky in Chicago, Benny began his career in vaudeville at 17. In 1932 he began hosting "The Jack Benny Show", a weekly radio program; it was tremendously popular, and ran for 23 years. He also performed on television and on stage.

Benson, Arthur Christopher (1862–1925). English author. Eldest son of the Archbishop of Canterbury, Benson taught at Eton and Cambridge. His works include poetry, novels, and essays, notably his 1902 essay *From a College Window*, critical studies, and biographies of his father and brother.

Berra, Yogi (1925-). American baseball player. Born Lawrence Peter Berra in St. Louis, Missouri, Berra began playing major league baseball in 1946. He was the New York Yankees' regular catcher through 1963. He established catcher's records for most home runs, and most consecutive errorless games. After retiring as a player, Berra managed and coached the Mets and the Yankees.

Blake, William (1757-1827). English poet and artist. Blake lived all his life in London. He was an engraver, and printed his poems and illustrations himself, using printing processes of his own invention. He was dismissed as an eccentric until long after his death, but his imaginative, mystical, metaphysical poems and art influenced English romanticism, and are widely acclaimed today. His works include *Songs of Innocence* and *Songs of Experience,* and *The Marriage of Heaven and Hell.*

Bok, Derek (1930–). American educator and university president. Born in Bryn Mawr, Pennsylvania, Bok became a professor of law at Harvard in 1958. He served as dean of the law school and then as president of the university. His books include *Beyond the Ivory Tower* and *The Trouble with Government.*

Bolton, Robert (1572-1631). English theologian. Bolton's books include *Of the Four Last Things, A Discourse on Happiness,* and *Instructions Relative to Afflicted Consciences.* They provide spiritual guidance and comfort.

Bonhoeffer, Dietrich (1906-45). German theologian. Born in Breslau, Germany, Bonhoeffer studied in Tubingen and in New York. When he returned to Germany Bonhoeffer began lecturing on theology in Berlin and wrote several books. A strong opponent of fascism, Bonhoeffer left Germany when Hitler gained power, but eventually returned to join the struggle as part of the anti-Nazi Confessional Church. With the outbreak of the war, Bonhoeffer's seminary was shut down by the Gestapo and he was banned from preaching, but he continued to work against Hitler. In 1943 Bonhoeffer was arrested and taken to Buchenwald Concentration Camp. He was executed in 1945. His *Ethics* and *Letters from Prison* were published after his death.

Borge, Victor (1909-2000). Danish-American pianist and comedian. While training to be a concert pianist at conservatories in his native Copenhagen, Vienna, and Berlin, Borge discovered he also had a talent for comedy. He began putting on entertaining shows that combined satire, physical comedy, and wordplay with his masterful piano playing. Borge, who was Jewish, fled the Nazis in 1940. He performed on radio, and held concerts at Carnegie Hall. His *Comedy in Music,* which ran for 839 performances, set a Broadway record for a one-man show. In 1963 Borge helped create a scholarship foundation for Scandinavian students, in gratitude to the many Scandinavian who helped the Jews during the Holocaust. His performance career spanned 70 years.

Bradley, Marion Zimmer (1930-99). American science fiction and fantasy writer. Marion Zimmer Bradley was born in Albany, New York. A science fiction fan as a teenager, she began writing stories for science fiction magazines in 1952. One of the few prominent women writers of science fiction, she is the author of the popular *Darkover* series. Her recent work includes books in the fantasy genre, such as *The Mists of Avalon,* based on Arthurian legend.

Bradley, Omar (1893-1981). American general. Born in Clark, Missouri, Bradley served in World War I. In World War II, Bradley led the invasion of Normandy and later commanded the U.S. 12th Army Group, the largest force ever commanded by a field commander, in the battle for Germany. He later became the first permanent Chairman of the Joint Chiefs of Staff.

Brontë, Anne (1820–49). English novelist. Daughter of an Anglican clergyman, Anne Brontë grew up in Yorkshire with her brother and two older sisters. Their mother died when Anne was an infant, and the Brontë children, left much to themselves, began to write about an imaginary world. All three sisters grew up to be gifted writers. They had to struggle to keep the family afloat financially as their father grew old and their brother declined into alcoholism and opium addiction. In 1846 the three sisters published their collected poems at their own expense, under male pseudonyms. In 1847 each sister published a novel – Anne's was *Agnes Grey.* In 1848 Anne published *the Tenant of Wildfel Hall.* Her brother and her sister Emily died of tuberculosis that same year; in 1849 Anne died of the same illness. Anne Brontë's novels, though not as acclaimed as her sisters', are admired for their realism and moral force.

Brown, Rita Mae. (1944-) American writer. Born in Hanover, Pennsylvania, Brown attended New York University. A political activist for feminist and lesbian causes Brown was an early member of the National Organization for Women. Her first novel, *Rubyfruit Jungle*, was published in 1973.

Browning, Robert. (1812-1889). English poet. Raised by well-read, ethical, artistic parents, Browning's education mostly took place at home, particularly in his father's huge library. He was an extremely precocious and voracious reader. He began his career by writing for the stage, then turned to dramatic monologues and long narrative poems. He lived in Italy for many years with his much-beloved wife, the poet Elizabeth Barrett Browning. Recognition for his poetry came slowly, but after the 1869 publication of *The Ring and the Book*, a twelve-book poem that tells the story of a 17th-century Roman murder from several different points of view, he was acclaimed as a great poet.

Bryan, William Jennings (1860–1925). American political leader. Bryan was a lawyer, a Nebraska Congressman, and a newspaper editor. He ardently promoted free and unlimited coinage of silver, which he believed would solve the economic problems of farmers and laborers. He played a prominent role in Democratic national conventions from 1896 to 1912, winning the presidential nomination three times. He served as Secretary of State under Woodrow Wilson. After his time, the nation adopted many of the reforms he had advocated, such as income tax, popular election of senators, and women's suffrage.

Buck, Pearl S. (1892-1973). American novelist. Born Pearl Sydenstriker in Hillsboro, West Virginia, she was the daughter of missionaries. Until 1933, she lived primarily in China. She wrote 85 books about China and its people. In novels such as *The Good Earth* Buck portrays Chinese life with vivid detail and warm sympathy. She won the Nobel Prize in literature in 1938. She assigned most of her royalties to charities she founded to help the children of Asian women and American soldiers.

Buddha (c.563-c.483 B.C.) Buddha is the title given to Siddhartha Gautama, the founder of Buddhism. Born the son of a king in what is now Nepal, Siddhartha forsook the luxury of palace life at 29, and left his wife and son to become a wandering ascetic. After years of yogic meditation, fasting and austerities, he seated himself under a pipal tree and meditated until he had attained supreme enlightenment at the age of 35. He spent the rest of his life traveling and living in a community of monks, teaching his doctrines of the "four noble truths" and the "eightfold path" to all who sought him out, regardless of their caste or religion.

Bulwer-Lytton, Edward (1831–91), English diplomat and poet. Son of a novelist, Bulwer-Lytton was a diplomat who served as viceroy of India and later ambassador to France. He was made an Earl for his service in the Afghan wars. He originally wrote under a pseudonym, Owen Meredith. His works include the 1858 collection *The Wanderer* and 1892's *King Poppy*, an epic fantasy.

Burns, Robert (1759-1796). Scottish poet. The son of a poor tenant farmer, Burns had to work hard in his youth. Nonetheless, he had a good grounding in English literature and Scottish poetry, thanks to his hardworking father, who tutored his sons at home and provided for as much additional education as possible. Burns published *Poems, Chiefly in the Scottish Dialect* in 1786. It was an immediate success. Burns then traveled the highlands, gathering songs for a collection of Scottish folksongs. Many of the songs were adapted from by Burns from traditional lyrics; some, such as "A Red, Red Rose," had wholly original lyrics. His are some of the best-loved poems in English.

Bussy-Rabutin, Roger de (1618-93). French aristocrat and writer. Born in Burgundy, De Bussy fought on both sides of the civil wars of the Fronde. He rose in military rank until 1665, when the unauthorized printing of his amusing but scandalous stories about court ladies, *Histoire amoureuse des Gaules,* landed him in jail.

Caird, Mona (1854-1932). English writer. Caird was the author of seven novels as well as journalism and pamphlets dealing with social and political questions She was controversial at the turn of the century for her advocacy of women's rights, civil liberties, and animal rights.

Camus, Albert (1913–60). French writer. Born and raised in Algiers, Camus went to Paris as a journalist in 1939. In World War II he was part of the French resistance. His philosophical novels, plays, and essays soon won him recognition as an important writer. Often called an existentialist for his belief in the absurdity of the human condition, Camus did not see himself as such. His works do not express despair so much as a courageous humanism and rebellion. His essay *The Myth of Sisyphus* and novel *The Stranger* are two of his best-known works.

Carlyle, Thomas (1795-1881). British historian and essayist. Born in the Scottish village of Ecclefechen, Carlyle studied at the University of Edinburgh. His father, a strict Calvinist, intended him to enter the ministry. Carlyle suffered several years of doubt and spiritual struggle before abandoning this idea, eventually settling on a literary career. His first major work was *Sartor Resaurtus,* his spiritual autobiography. In 1834 he began *The French Revolution.* Carlyle saw history as "Divine Scripture", and treated the revolution as judgment upon the corruption of the monarchy. Full of well-documented detail, fiery, dramatic narrative, and memorable portraits, the book is also memorable for its poetic and meditations on humanity and history. In 1835, he lent the first volume to John Stuart Mill, who accidentally burned it in his fireplace. Carlyle lost many months of work, and was suffering from poverty. Normally an irritable man, he could rise to major challenges, and reacted to this loss with grace. *The French Revolution* was published in 1837, and its success made Carlyle's career. As a lecturer and writer on government, religion, economics, and history, he became one of the most influential social critics of his day. His wife, whose ambition and intelligence had been important to Carlyle's career, died in 1866, and this loss cast a shadow on the rest of his life.

Carnegie. Andrew (1835–1919). American industrialist. Born in Scotland, son of a factory worker, Carnegie came to Alleghany (now Pittsburgh), Pennsylvania with his family in 1848. He first worked a bobbin boy in a cotton mill, then as a telegrapher, and in 1859 became a superintendent for the Pennsylvania RR. Carnegie invested in iron manufactures. In 1873, Carnegie began to acquire firms that produced steel, which were later consolidated into the Carnegie Steel Company. By 1900, the Carnegie Steel Company was producing one quarter of all the steel in the United States and controlled iron mines, coke ovens, ore ships, and railroads. In 1901 Carnegie sold the company and retired. Carnegie's essay "The Gospel of Wealth" (1889) expressed his belief that rich men should use their wealth for the good of the public. As a philanthropist he established many cultural institutions, including Carnegie Hall in New York City and over 2,800 libraries.

Carter, Hodding (1907–72). American journalist. Born in Hammond, Louisiana, Carter became a spokesman for the progressive "New South". He wrote a series of editorials on racial, economic, and religious intolerance that won the 1946 Pulitzer Prize. He founded two newspapers, one of which, the *Delta Democrat-Times,* he edited for over 30 years. His books include *The Angry Scar: The Story of Reconstruction* and *First Person Rural.*

Cato the Elder (234–149 B.C.). Roman statesman and moralist. Marcus Portius Cato, known as Cato the Elder or Cato the Censor, fought in the Second Punic War and served as a magistrate. He was renowned for his devotion to the old Roman ideals—simplicity of life, honesty, and unflinching courage. A great orator and a prolific and influential writer, his only surviving work, *De agri cultura* or *De re rustica,* is a treatise on farming

Chanel, Coco (1883–1971). French fashion designer. Born in the village of Samaur, Chanel spent time in an orphange after her mother died and her father left. The nuns that had cared for her found her a job as a seamstress when she was 17, but she left it to try for a career as a cabaret singer. When that failed, she moved to Paris and opened a milliner's shop. She established a house of couture, selling clothes that were simple rather than ostentatious, and introduced elements previously exclusive to men's clothes – trousers, humble materials such as jersey, loose-fitting sweaters. She was and remains an enormously influential designer.

Chaplin, S. (1916-86). English writer. The son of a coal miner, Sidney Chaplin entered the mines at 15. He continued to work as a miner while obtaining an education through workers' associations and colleges. Chaplin first gained a reputation as a writer with 1946's *The Leaping Lad*, a short story collection about the Durham mining community.

Charles, Elizabeth (1828-1896). English writer. Born in Devon, Elizabeth Charles (née Rundle) was the author of many popular religious novels, including *The Chronicles of the Schonberg-Cotta Family*, based on the life of Martin Luther. She also wrote several hymns, and founded a hospice in London.

Cher (1946-). American actress and singer. Born Cherilyn LaPiere Sarkisian in El Centro, California, Cher met Sonny Bono, a record producer, in a coffee shop when she was 16. The two began performing together as a musical act, and married when Cher was 18. In the 1970s, they starred in two television variety shows, one before, and one after, their divorce in 1974. In the 80s, Cher began a successful career as a film actress.

Chesterton, G. K. (1874-1936). English writer. Born and educated in London, Chesterton was popular for his witty writing, although also controversial for his extreme religious and political conservatism. Chesterton's many writings include literary criticism, collections of poetry, and theological works, novels and the popular Father Brown detective series.

Chopin, Frédéric (1810–49). Polish composer. Born near Warsaw to a French father and Polish mother, Chopin began studying piano at age four. A prodigy as a pianist and as a composer, he performed at aristocratic salons as a child, and in 1826 entered the Warsaw Conservatory. He eventually settled in Paris, where he taught, composed, and performed. He never returned to his war-torn homeland, but he remained deeply attached to it. The influence of Polish folk music can be heard in his works. His last concert was a benefit for Polish refugees, and when he died in Paris of tuberculosis in 1849, Polish soil was sprinkled on his grave. Chopin's compositions, which are nearly all for piano, are romantic and lyrical.

Churchill, Winston (1874-1965). English statesman. The son of a prominent Tory politician, Churchill had a lonely, neglected boyhood. A poor student, he embarked on an army career. He served in the South African war and in India as both a soldier and a journalist. His dispatches from the front, appearing in the *Morning Post*, brought him fame. In 1900 he was elected to Parliament. As Lord of the Admiralty, he helped prepare the Navy for World War I. As Colonial Secretary, he helped negotiate the establishment of the Irish Free State. Out of office from 1929, Churchill maintained a voice in public affairs. In his writings, he warned against the Nazi threat. He reentered government at the outbreak of World War II, and became Prime Minister in 1940. Along with Roosevelt and Stalin, he shaped the strategy of the Allies. A great orator, his steadfast resistance to compromise with Hitler rallied the spirits of the British during the difficult times of the war. After the war, he alerted the west to the expansionist threat of the Soviet Union. A leader of energy, resolve, imagination, and boldness, Churchill was one of the great statesmen of the 20th century.

Cicero (106 B.C.–43 B.C.). Roman orator, politician and philosopher. Cicero studied law and philosophy at Rome, Athens, and Rhodes, and served in several government positions. He sought to defend the republic, and was an enemy of Caeser. He was put to death by Octavian. Cicero's voluminous writings include philosophical works, rhetorical works, orations, and letters. His letters reveal more of Roman life and political manners than does any other source. His orations have become the standard of Latin. Cicero's style is very pure, and he is a master of Latin prose.

Clay, Henry (1777-1852). Born in Virginia, Clay made a reputation as a lawyer and orator in Kentucky. He served in state legislature, and in Congress, where he was Speaker of the House. He was John Quincy Adams' secretary of state, and a U.S. Senator during the Jackson administration. Skilled in the art of political compromise, Clay was known as the "Great Pacificator" for his role in the Missouri Compromise and in resolving other political conflicts.

Coleridge, Samuel Taylor (1772-1834). English poet. Precocious and imaginative from a young age, Coleridge spent his childhood immersed in romances and exotic tales such as *Arabian Nights*. He impressed his schoolmates with his eloquence and erudition. He left Cambridge University in his third year, planning to found a utopian community with the poet Robert Southey. This plan came to nothing. A few years later, Coleridge met the poet William Wordsworth. Coleridge was already writing poetry, but his friendship with Wordsworth marked the beginning of his best work. Together, they wrote *Lyrical Ballads*, which heralded the English Romantic movement. "The Rime of the Ancient Mariner"was Coleridge's main contribution to this volume. Coleridge's *Biographia Literaria*, is a mixture of autobiography, critical writing, and a theory of the creative imagination. This last is one of Coleridge's greatest concerns, and is linked to another frequent theme of his poetry, his religious idea of the "life-consciousness" of individuals, and the wonder present in the world.

Colette (1873–1954). French novelist. Born Sidonie-Gabrielle Colette in the Burgundian village of Saint-Sauveur-en Puisaye, she spent a happy childhood in rural surroundings, later the scene of many of her novels. She began her writing career at the age of 20 with the publication of the wildly popular *Claudine* series of novels, the first of which was *Claudine at School*. Colette wrote prolifically all her life, remaining a popular and critically esteemed writer. She was the first woman admitted to the prestigious Goncourt Academy and the second to become a grand officer of the French Legion of Honor. Colette was a fiercely independent woman. Her semi-autobiographical novels, intimate in tone, explore the lives of women.

Commoner, Barry (1917-). American scientist and activist. A biologist who first became prominent in the 1950s, when he pushed for atmospheric testing of nuclear weapons, Commoner has gone on to a long career of activism on environmental and social issues. In his writings and activism, he emphasizes the connection between social inequality and environmental destruction. His books include *Science and Survival*, *The Closing Circle*, and *Making Peace with the Planet*.

Conant, James Bryant (1893–1978). American chemist, educator, and diplomat. Conant was a professor of chemistry and later University president at Harvard. As director of the National Defense Research Committee during World War II, Conant played a significant role in the development of the atomic bomb. In 1953 he was appointed U.S. High Commissioner for Germany and later served as ambassador to West Germany. Later he conducted extensive studies of American public high schools, and became one of the most prominent critics of American education. His writings on that subject include *Education and Liberty*, and *Slums and Suburbs*.

Connery, Sean (1930-). Scottish actor. Born in Edinburgh, Scotland, Connery became famous when he played the role of James Bond in a series of spy movies. He won an Academy award for his role in *The Untouchables*.

Cooley, Mason. (1927-). American writer. Cooley is the author of *City Aphorisms*.

Coolidge, Calvin (1872–1933). United States president. Born in Plymouth, Vermont, John Calvin Coolidge graduated from Amherst College and practiced law in Northampton, Massachusetts. He held a variety of state offices and in 1920 was elected to the vice presidency along with President Harding. Coolidge became president in 1923 after Harding died, and was easily elected to a full term in 1924. He was popular for his honesty and New England simplicity, and for his conservative, pro-business values. After leaving office he retired to Northampton to write newspaper and magazine articles and his autobiography.

Cosby, Bill (1937-). American actor, comedian. Born in Philadelphia, Cosby first became known as a comedian. He was the first African-American to star in a television series, and has won many Emmy Awards. He has written several books, including *Fatherhood*. Cosby is also known for his public service.

Cousins, Norman (1912–90). American editor, author. The editor of The Saturday Review for over a quarter of a century, Norman Cousins has written books on politics, society, and health. His works include *Anatomy of an Illness*, an autobiographical account that emphasizes the power of the mind over the body. He has been a Professor of Medical Humanities at the UCLA School of Medicine.
Cowper, William (1731-1800). English poet. Born in Hertfordshire,

England, Cowper was the son of an Anglican minister. In 1754, he became a barrister, but shortly afterwards experienced his first attack of mental illness. For the rest of his life, he would suffer from mental instability and delicate physical health. He sought solace in religion, at one point attempting to become an evangelist, but ultimately found poetry to be his one unfailing refuge. Cowper's poetry described the fields and hedgerows of rural England, and the joys and sorrows of everyday life. This ordinary subject matter, along with his relatively simple language, brought a new directness to 18th century poetry. Cowper, whose poems include *The Task*, was one of the most popular poets of his day.

cummings, e.e. (1894–1962). American poet. Born Edward Estlin Cumming in Cambridge, Massachusetts, he attended Harvard University from 1911 to 1916. His study of modernists such as Gertrude Stein and Pablo Picasso was reflected in his own formally experimental poetry, which he began to publish at this time. Cummings' playful, often humorous and life-affirming verse experiments wildly with punctuation, spelling, language and sentence structure. He had difficulty getting his work published throughout his life, but today is an extremely popular poet. Cummings also had a career as a painter. *The Enormous Room*, his prose account of his internment in France, is considered one of the best books about World War I.

Dante Alighieri (1265–1321). Italian poet. Born in Florence, Dante moved in patrician society. After the death in 1290 of Beatrice, the woman he loved, he plunged into intense study of classical philosophy and Provençal poetry. Beatrice was Dante's inspiration, and his c.1292 collection of prose and lyrics *La vita nuova* is written in praise of her and reflects Dante's vision of ideal love. Dante was active in the politics of Florence; in 1302 he was exiled, and from then on served various Italian princes. During his exile, Dante composed the *Divine Comedy*, a long vernacular poem that recounts the poet's journey through Hell, Purgatory, and Heaven. The *Divine Comedy* employs complex symbolism and musical verse to treat religious and philosophical themes. It is one of the greatest and most influential works of literature.

Darrow, Clarence (1857–1938). American lawyer. Born in Kinsman, Ohio, Darrow resigned his position of general counsel for the Chicago and Northwestern Railroad in 1894 to defend Eugene V. Debs and others involved in the Pullman strike. Later, he gave up a lucrative law practice to champion the causes he believed in. An opponent of the death penalty, he took on over 100 murder defenses; none of his clients was ever sentenced to death. Darrow is best remembered for the 1925 Scopes trial, which was portrayed in the movie *Inherit the Wind*; he defended a schoolteacher charged with breaking Tennessee law by teaching evolution.

Davies, Robertson (1913-95). Canadian writer. Born in Ontario, Davies was educated there and at Oxford University in England. He became an actor, then editor and publisher of an Ontario newspaper, and an English professor. He is known for three trilogies of novels that employ diverse approaches – comedy, satire, allegory, historical romance – to describe Canadian life.

de Bono, Edward (1933-). Italian educator, motivational speaker, and author. Born in Malta, de Bono has written numerous books and worked with many corporations and other organizations on the topics of creativity, leadership, and cognition.

De Bury, Richard (1287–1345) English bishop and bibliophile. De Bury served as treasurer and as chancellor to Edward III . He founded a library and wrote *Philobiblon*, an autobiographical account of book-collecting.

de Mille, Agnes (1905–93). American choreographer and dancer. Born in New York City to a theatrical family, de Mille moved to Europe and worked on ballets. Returning to America, she brought ballet form to the musical theatre in her choreography of shows such as *Oklahoma!*, *Brigadoon,* and *Carousel.* As the choreographer of some 15 musicals and 21 ballets, de Mille did much to popularize serious dance with the public.

Delille, Jacques (1738-1813). French abbé and poet. Delille's well-received verse translations of Virgil earned him a place in the French Academy. Forced to leave France after the Revolution, he returned in 1802, and published his own verses, highly praised in his day.

Dickens, Charles (1812–70). English author. The son of a naval clerk, Dickens spent his early childhood in London and in Chatham. When he was 12 his father was imprisoned for debt, and Dickens was compelled to work in a blacking warehouse. He later worked as a

261

journalist, an experience which informed his life as a writer of social novels and campaigner for social issues. In 1833 he began publishing popular sketches of London life in periodicals. He became famous with the publication of the *Pickwick Papers*, a collection of humorous sketches about a group of eccentric characters. Dickens' reputation and popularity only grew greater with time. He worked hard to please his many eager readers, prolifically turning out novels in monthly installments. Dickens used his own life as a source for many novels, particularly *David Copperfield*. Sharp and vivid in their depictions of characters and places, intricately plotted, and filled with human feeling, Dickens' novels form a richly textured world.

Dickinson, Emily (1830–86). American poet. The middle child of a prominent lawyer, Emily Dickinson lived in the Amherst, Massachusetts house where she was born for almost her entire life. She was the author of over 2,000 poems, but had little interest in publishing them; only 10 were printed in her lifetime. She kept up a large correspondence with friends, especially her sister-in-law, with whom she was very close. Many of her poems deal with her spiritual questioning, alternating between expressions of faith and doubt and despair. Her poetry is unique: witty, imagistic, and direct, and rich in thought and feeling. She is one of the greatest American poets.

Dimnet, Ernest. (1866-1954). French writer. Dimnet, ordained in 1893, was a professor of English literature in Paris. He wrote literary criticism, religious studies, autobiographies, and the popular *Art of Thinking*.

Disraeli, Benjamin (1804–81). British statesman and author. Disraeli was of Jewish ancestry, but his father, the literary critic Isaac D'Israeli, had him baptized in 1817. Disraeli was a prolific author of novels and political essays. He was elected to Parliament as a Tory in 1837, and quickly became a highly skilled politician famed for his keen wit and sharp tongue. He opposed free trade legislation, and got the Reform Bill of 1867 passed, enfranchising about 2 million workingmen. Disraeli was prime minister in 1868, and from 1874 to 1880. His administration enacted many domestic reforms in housing, public health, and factory legislation. Disraeli pursued an aggressive foreign policy, waging war all over the world to consolidate the Empire. He is seen as the founder of the modern Conservative party.

Dochez, Alphonse Raymond (1882-1964). American scientist. Born in

San Francisco of Belgian parentage, Dochez was a bacteriologist at the Rockefeller Institute for Medical Research, Johns Hopkins, and Columbia University. He made notable discoveries about the bacteria that cause infectious diseases such as pneumonia and scarlet fever.

Donne, John (1572-1631). English poet and clergyman. Born in London, Donne entered Oxford at age 11, and also studied at Cambridge and Lincoln's Inn. After participating in a naval expedition against Spain, Donne became secretary to Sir Thomas Egerton, Lord Keeper of the Great Seal, and began to make a reputation as a poet. His unsanctioned marriage to Sir Thomas Egerton's niece ended Donne's career at court. After years of making a meager living as a lawyer, Donne became a clergyman. Famed for the eloquence of his sermons, he was made a royal chaplain and dean of St. Paul's Cathedral. Donne is considered the greatest of the metaphysical poets, and a great love poet. In poems such as "the Ecstasie" he connects the two strains, finding the roots of spiritual love in physical love. In contrast to the elegant, sentimental love sonnets of his day, Donne's wider view of love includes passion, realism, and even cynicism.

Douglass, Frederick (1818-1895). American writer, activist. Author of the most famous slave narrative ever written, Frederick Douglass escaped slavery to become one of the most important thinkers, writers and political figures in American history. Douglass was born Frederick Augustus Bailey, the slave of one Aaron Anthony on Maryland's Eastern Shore, the son of Harriet Bailey, a slave, and an unknown white man. In 1838 he escaped to the north and joined the abolitionist movement, penning the now famous story of his life, speaking out against slavery and editing the abolitionist newspaper, *The North Star*. A radical democrat in every sense, Douglass would become a tireless supporter of the women's rights movement. He died in 1895 a few hours after delivering a stirring speech at a women's rights rally.

Douglas, William O. (1898-1980). American jurist. As chairman of the Security and Exchange Commission, Douglas worked hard to protect small investors through government regulation. A supporter of the New Deal, he was appointed to the Supreme Court by Franklin Delano Roosevelt in 1939. In his 36-year tenure, he was a consistent defender of civil liberties, particularly of the First Amendment guarantees of freedom of speech and of the press. He also wrote prolifically on conservation, history, and politics.

DuBois, W.E.B. (1868-1963). American philsopher, novelist and activist. Dubois was born in Great Barrington, Massachusetts, a small village with only a handful of black families. He would go on to become the nation's most profound philsopher of race relations. Having studied with WillIam James at Harvard, DuBois published *The Souls of Black Folk* in 1903, arguing that 'the problem of the Twentieth century is the problem of the color-line.' DuBois played a pivotal role in the Niagra Movement which in 1910 became the NAACP. As a leader in the NAACP he would edit its official organ, *The Crisis*. DuBois's politics grew increasingly radical causing friction with his own organization. He organized several Pan-African congresses in New York and Europe in an attempt to combat colonialism and in 1963 he renounced his American citizenship, becoming a citizen of Ghana.

Dylan, Bob (1941-). American singer-songwriter. Born Robert Allen Zimmerman in Duluth, Minnesota, Dylan learned guitar at the age of ten and autoharp and harmonica at 15. After a rebellious youth, he moved to New York City in 1960. Influenced by American roots music, Dylan had an enormous effect on folk and rock. His lyrics expressed the anger and convictions of the times, as did his raw, insistent singing and guitar playing. His protest songs include "Blowin' in the Wind" and "The Times They Are A-Changin'." Dylan continues to tour and produce new albums.

Earhart, Amelia (1897–1937). American aviator. Driven by a passion for aviation from the time she saw an air show as a young woman, Earhart saved money from her salary as a social worker to pay for flying lessons and eventually her own airplane. In 1928 she became the first woman to cross the Atlantic by airplane, and in 1932 the first woman to make a solo flight across the Atlantic. She was also the first person to fly alone from Honolulu to California. In 1937, while attempting to fly around the world, her plane was lost on the flight between New Guinea and Howland Island.

Edison, Thomas A. (1847-1931). American inventor. Born in Milan, Ohio, Thomas Edison only received three months of schooling. At age 12, he began work as a newsboy, and later became a telegraph operator. Several of his first inventions were telegraph devices. With the proceeds from his inventions, Edison set up workshops in New Jersey. These workshops, with their teams of workers, set the pattern for the modern industrial research laboratory. Edison patented over a thousand inventions in his lifetime, including the mimeograph, the carbon telephone transmitter, the phonograph, the incandescent electric lamp, the alkaline battery, and talking motion pictures. Edison was one of the greatest and most prolific inventors of his time.

Edwards, Robert C. (1864-1922). Canadian newspaper editor. Edwards was the colorful editor and publisher of the *Calgary Eye-Opener*.

Ehrmann, Max (1872-1945). Born in Terre Haute, Indiana to Bavarian immigrants, Ehrmann worked as an attorney until the age 40, when he turned to writing full-time. He is famous for *Desiderata*, a long inspirational poem that offers advice for living.

Eliot, George (1819-1880). Born Mary Ann Evans, Eliot left boarding school at 17 to care for her widowed father. From then on, she educated herself, reading assiduously. In 1841 she began reading rationalist works and rejected the dogmatic evangelical faith in which she had been raised. After the death of her father, she began to write reviews and articles under the pseudonym George Eliot, becoming an assistant editor at the *Westminster Review*. There she met many of the leading literary figures of the day, including George Lewes, with whom she fell in love. Eliot braved social ostracism to live with Lewes, whom she could not marry because his estranged wife was still living. Lewes encouraged her to write fiction and was extremely supportive and protective of Eliot and her work. Impressive in scope, Eliot's novels offer a broad and detailed portrait of the social world in which Eliot grew up, that of English provincial towns. They are even more remarkable for their portrayal of their characters' inner lives, which Eliot described with an attention and psychological insight never before seen in English literature. Eliot's novels include *Middlemarch* and *Silas Marner*.

Eliot, T.S. (1888-1965). American-British poet and critic. Born in St. Louis, Missouri, to an old New England family, Eliot received a wide education. He settled in London, eventually becoming a British subject. His first important poem, 1915's *The Love Song of J. Alfred Prufrock*, represented a break from the immediate past and the rise of modernism in English poetry. Eliot won an international reputation with the 1922 publication of *The Waste Land*. This extremely complex poem expresses the disillusionment and despair of the post-World War I world. Eliot's criticism, which asserted the impersonality of great art, and the poet's claim to the whole of literary tradition, did as much to revolutionize 20th century literature as his formally innovative poetry. Eliot was confirmed into the Church of England in 1927. In his later work, he turns from spiritual desolation to hope for salvation through religion.

Elliot, John Jr. (1948-). American businessman. Born in Charlotte, North Carolina, Elliot is the president of a chemical company.

Ellis, Havelock (1859-1939). English psychologist and writer. Ellis gave up a medical practice to devote himself to writing and scientific research. A pioneer in the field of sexual psychology, he is best known for his seven-volume work *Studies in the Psychology of Sex.* He is also the author of poems, essays, and an autobiography, *My Life,* which focuses on his marriage.

Ellison, Ralph (1914-1994). American Writer. Born in Oklahoma City, Ellison showed an early love for music and immersed himself in the jazz culture of the Southwest, hearing in person such legends as King Oliver and Count Basie. In 1933 he entered the Tuskegee Institute for conservatory training. Leaving after his Junior year, Ellison set off for New York City where he would meet such writers as Langston Hughes and Richard Wright, work on the Federal Writers Project and transform himself into a novelist. Indeed, he would write one of the great novels of the twentieth century, *Invisible Man* published in 1952. Ellison was also a superb essayist, writing on a wide variety of topics from art, music, literature and culture and publishing his essays in two collections. His posthumous second novel, *Juneteenth,* was published in 1999.

Emerson, Ralph Waldo (1803-82). American writer. Born in Boston, Emerson, like his father, was a Unitarian minister. In 1832 he resigned as pastor of a Boston Church because of theological differences with his congregation. He then traveled in Europe, where he met such writers as Carlyle and Wordsworth; English Romanticism was to be an important influence on his thought. Emerson settled in Concord, Massachusetts, and began giving public lectures and writing. His 1836 book *Nature* put forth his transcendentalist philosophy, which, in opposition to organized religion, sought spirituality in nature and within the individual. Emerson also emphasized the importance of self-reliance and freedom of the individual. Emerson and other New England intellectuals founded a transcendentalist journal, *The Dial,* which Emerson edited for several years. He continued to publish essays and poems, and became famous through his lecture tours. He also became active in the abolitionist movement, delivering many passionate speeches in favor of Emancipation and raising funds for the Massachusetts 54th Regiment, the first black regiment to fight in the Civil War whom Emerson memorialized in his poem 'Voluntaries.' Emerson has had a major influence on American thought.

Ennius, Quintus (239-c.169 B.C.). Roman poet. Born in Calabria, Ennius met Cato the elder in Sardinia, and accompanied him to Rome. There he made a living by teaching and translating Greek. His ambition was to be a Latin Homer, and his innovations in Latin poetry won him the status as the father of Roman poetry.

Epictetus (c.55-c.135), Greek philosopher. Born a slave in Phyrgia (now Turkey), Epictetus studied the philosophy of Stoicism in his youth. After his master freed him, Epictetus taught philosophy in Rome. He wrote nothing, but his teachings were recorded by his student Arrian in the *Discourses* and the *Encheiridion*. Epictetus emphasized morality, indifference to worldly goods, and the brotherhood of man.

Euripides (c.480 B.C.- 406 B.C.) Greek tragic dramatist. Although well known, the tragedies of Euripides were criticized during his lifetime for their unconventionality. More realistic than the plays of his contemporaries, they often dealt with ordinary people and human problems rather than heroic characters and mythic grandeur. His works, which include *The Bacchae* and *Medea*, became more popular after his death. Of his approximately 92 plays, 18 survive; they are considered classics, and have influenced European literature.

Faulkner, William (1897-1962). The grandson of a colorful Civil War colonel, Faulkner was raised in Oxford, Mississippi. He lived there, a rural recluse, even after achieving fame as a writer. The imaginary Yoknapatawpha county, the setting for most of his novels, is based on Oxford. Yoknapatawpha county, deep-rooted in the past, serves as a microcosm of the South. Faulkner's novels explore the passions and suffering of the rural South, and the blood ties as well as blood hatreds between black and white, rich and poor. His novels' stream-of-consciousness narrative, complex structure, and dense, rich language at first limited their commercial success, but eventually earned their recognition as some of the greatest, most influential works of modernist fiction. Faulkner won the Nobel Prize in 1949. His novels include *Absalom, Absalom* and *As I Lay Dying*.

Feather, William (1889-1981). American writer and publisher. Born in Jamestown, New York, Feather published a magazine for businessmen and was the author of numerous books and articles on achieving success in business.

Finley, John Huston (1863-1940). American educator, author, and editor. Born in Grand Ridge, Illinois, Finely became president of Knox University at the young age of 28. He later became the president of the City College of New York, and Commissioner of Education for the State of New York. He also served as editor of *Harper's Weekly,* and for two decades was an associate editor and frequent contributor to *The New York Times.* He wrote books on education, politics, and the humanities, and was active in philanthropies.

Fischer, Martin H. (1879-1962). German-born American physician. In addition to many scientific books, Fischer wrote biographies and books of aphorisms.

Fitzhenry, R. I. (1918-). American-born Canadian editor. Robert Fitzhenry is the editor of the popular *Harper Book of Quotations.* He is also a publisher.

Fletcher, Joseph (1905-91). American clergyman and author. Born in Newark, New Jersey, Fletcher, an Episcopalian minister, taught ethics for over 30 years. He is best remembered for his pioneering work in the field of medical ethics. Fletcher's many books include *Morals and Medicine* and *Situation Ethics.*

Fonda, Henry (1905–83). American actor. Born in Grand Island, Nebraska, Fonda became a star of both stage and screen. He is known for his portrayals of honest, decent men, in films such as *The Grapes of Wrath.* He was the father of Jane Fonda and Peter Fonda.

Ford, Gerald (1913-). United States president. Born Leslie Lynch King, Jr. in Omaha, Nebraska, Ford was renamed after his stepfather, who adopted him. Ford played on the University of Michigan's championship football team, and then worked full time as a coach at Yale while studying law there. Ford spent 25 years in the House of Representatives. He was appointed Nixon's vice president after Spiro Agnew resigned in 1973, and nine months later became president when Nixon resigned. Ford worked to restore the public faith that had been shattered by Watergate and to fight inflation and recession. These inherited problems, along with his controversial pardon of Nixon, contributed to his defeat in the presidential election of 1976.

Ford, Henry (1863-1947). American industrialist. Born in Dearborn, Michigan, Ford left his father's farm at age 16 to work as an apprentice in a Detroit machine shop. Later on, while an engineer at the Edison Illuminating Company, Ford constructed his first automobile in his spare time. In 1903 he founded the Ford Motor Company. Using assembly line production and standardized, interchangeable parts, Ford quickly became the largest automobile manufacturer in the world. As the industrialist most responsible for the general adoption of mass production, Ford played an important role in the expansion of industry in America.

Fosdick, Raymond B. (1883-1972). American lawyer. Born in Buffalo, New York, Fosdick began his career as counsel for the City of New York, acquiring a reputation as a reformer and a graft-buster. He was appointed the first undersecretary of the League of Nations in 1919. A fervent internationalist, Fosidick accepted the post without pay. When the Senate refused to allow the United States to join the League, he resigned in disappointment. He founded a law firm, and was very active in philanthropic work, eventually becoming president of the Rockefeller Foundation. Throughout his life Fosdick was an internationalist who worked hard to promote the League of Nations, a world court, and the United Nations as vehicles for peace. Fosdick was the author of 14 books, including his autobiography, *Chronicle of a Generation.*

France, Anatole (1844–1924). French writer. Probably the most prominent French man of letters of his time, France wrote in an elegant, subtly ironic style. Among his best-remembered works is *Penguin Island*, an allegorical novel satirizing French history. He won the 1921 Nobel Prize in Literature.

Francis de Sales, Saint (167-1622). French bishop. A member of an aristocratic Savoy family, St. Francis briefly practiced law before, against his father's wishes, he entered the priesthood. He spent his first years as a priest preaching to Protestants in Chablais, and converted many to Catholicism. He rose to become bishop of Geneva in 1602. He established many schools in his dioscese, and paid special attention to poor parishes. He is known for his *Introduction to the Devout Life* and other writings.

Franklin, Benjamin (1706–1790). American statesman, printer, scientist, and writer. Born in Boston, Franklin left school at age ten to help his father, a tallow chandler. In his spare time he read widely, and studied languages, philosophy, and science. He took up work as a printer, and eventually owned and edited a Pennsylvania newspaper, which became popular for Franklin's common sense philosophy and pithy phrases. From 1732 to 1757 Franklin published *Poor Richard's Almanack*, a compendium of sayings praising prudence, common sense, honesty, industry and thrift – values that guided Franklin's life and had helped him to better himself. In 1748 he gave up his printing business to devote his life to science. He conducted experiments that resulted in important discoveries regarding electricity. Ever practical, Franklin also invented bifocals, the Franklin stove, and other useful items. Franklin was deputy postmaster general of the colonies for over twenty years. He traveled to Britain to represent Pennsylvania's interests on a number of occasions. He became one of the greatest statesmen of the American Revolution and of the newborn nation. A delegate to the Continental Congress, and a member of the committee that drafted the Declaration of Independence, Franklin also acted as a diplomat, helping to gain French recognition of the new republic. He helped direct the compromise that brought the Constitution of the United States into being. Famed as a patriot, Franklin is also remembered for his writings, especially for his autobiography.

Frayn, Michael (1933-) English writer. Born in London, Frayn began his writing career as a reporter and columnist for the Manchester Guardian. He is the author of novels and plays, including the 1982 farce *Noises Off*, and *Copenhagen*, an investigation into uncertainty in science, history, and human motivation.

Fromm, Erich (1900–1980). American psychoanalyst. Born in Frankfurt, Fromm came to the United States in 1934. He practiced psychoanalysis and lectured at Columbia University and other institutions. Recognized as an important leader in psychoanalytic thought, Fromm broke with the traditional Freudian focus on unconscious motivations, maintaining that people are formed by their cultures. Fromm's many works include *Escape from Freedom, The Sane Society* and *To Have or to Be*.

Frost, Robert (1874–1963). American poet. Frost grew up in Lawrence, Massachussetts, where his family had lived for generations. After briefly studying at Dartmouth and Harvard, and working as a cobbler, a bobbin boy in a cotton mill, a schoolteacher, and a farmer, Frost and his wife and children moved to England in search of literary success. There he published two collections of poems. Frost's poetry uses the language, life, and landscape of rural New England. After two years in England, he returned to America a popular poet. He lived on a farm, taught and lectured, and wrote poetry for the rest of his life. He won four Pulitzer Prizes, and in 1961 read his poem "The Gift Outright" at John F. Kennedy's presidential inauguration.

Fuentes, Carlos (1928–). Mexican writer and diplomat. Born in Panama City, Fuentes, the son of a diplomat, spent time in North and South America and Europe. From 1956 to 1959 he was head of the department of cultural relations in Mexico's ministry of foreign affairs, and was the Mexican ambassador to France from 1975 to 1977. In the 1950's Fuentes began publishing short stories. His 1962 novel *The Death of Artemio Cruz* won him international fame. In his many novels and essays, Fuentes imaginatively deals with Mexican history, culture, and identity. His writing has had a strong influence on contemporary Latin American literature.

Fulghum, Robert (1937-). American writer. Born in Waco, Texas, Fulghum is a Unitarian minister. He began writing down his daily insights for use in sermons and Church newsletters. Soon photocopies of his inspirational essays were circulating within the Unitarian community. A literary agent read one, and approached Fulghum about writing a book. *All I Really Need to Know I Learned in Kindergarten,* with its humor, simplicity, and insight, proved to be tremendously popular with the American public.

Fuller, Thomas (1608-61). English clergyman and author. Educated at Cambridge, Fuller became a preacher in London. He served as a chaplain to the Royalist army and to the household of the infant princess Henrietta during the Civil War. A witty writer, his many historical works were notable for their character sketches and richness of detail. His 1622 *Histories of the Worthies of England* was the first dictionary of national biography.

Galbraith, J.K. (1908–). American economist. Born in Ontario, Canada, Galbraith has worked as an economics professor, an editor of *Fortune* magazine, and in government service. Galbraith was a personal an advisor to President Kennedy and U.S. ambassador to India. In addition to his academic work, he has written influential and popular books on politics, economics, and culture for the general public, including *The Affluent Society* and *The Great Crash*.

Gandhi, Mohandas K. (1869-1948). Indian political and spiritual leader. Born in Porbandar, Gandhi studied law in England and practiced in India and South Africa. He remained in South Africa for 20 years, struggling for the rights of the Indian community there. Influenced by wide reading, including the Baghvad Gita, Tolstoy, and Thoreau, Gandhi developed a philosophy whose tenets included an ascetic way of life and *satyaghara*. Sanskrit for "holding to the truth", *satyaghara* was Gandhi's term for the campaigns of nonviolent civil resistance he organized. After the South African government granted many of the rights the Indian community had sought, Gandhi returned to India. There he became a leader in the campaign for home rule. Millions of Indians joined his campaigns of nonviolent resistance against the British colonial government. Gandhi also campaigned against economic exploitation by the British, encouraging home industries and the boycott of British goods. Besides freedom from British rule, Gandhi wanted a united India and the abolition of caste and untouchability. Gandhi's ideas had enormous influence, and to Indians, his moral stature was such that he was called "Mahatma", or great soul. He was imprisoned many times, but because of his enormous importance to people in India and around the world, the British ultimately had to free him and heed his demands. Indian independence was granted in 1947, and, though Gandhi strongly opposed it, a separate state of Pakistan was carved out for Muslims. Gandhi traveled the country seeking to calm the violence between Hindus and Muslims that broke out during the partition of the country. In 1948 he was assassinated by a Hindu fanatic who resented his religious tolerance. His teachings have inspired nonviolent movements around the world.

Garbo, Greta (1905-90). American film actress. Born Greta Gustaffson in Stockholm, Garbo came to Hollywood following her success in the Swedish film *The Atonement of Gösta Berling*. Renowned for her beauty, Garbo became known for playing tragic heroines in films such as *Anna Karenina* and *Queen Christina*. She retired in 1941 and lived a secluded life from then on.

Geneen, Harold (1910-1997). American businessman . Born in Britain, Geneen came to America as an infant. He began his career as an accountant, and, propelled by his attention to financial detail, self-confidence, and toughness, rose to the top of several corporations. In 1959, he began an 18-year stint as CEO of International Telephone & Telegraph, which he transformed into one of America's biggest firms. Geneen is credited with inventing the concept of the conglomerate, and his business model was used by many other firms.

Gibran, Khalil (1883–1931). Lebanese writer. Gibran moved to New York City in 1912. He became famous for his poetic, aphoristic works drawing on the wisdom of the world's religions, such as *The Prophet.*
Gide, André (1869–1951). French writer. He established his reputation with his partially autobiographical novel *The Immoralist*. Like many of his novels, it tells the story of an individual who crosses the boundaries of conventional morality in his quest for self-realization. Gide became a leader of French liberal thought. His many writings include plays, stories, and essays on a wide variety of subjects. His *Travels in the Congo* and *Retour du Tchad* helped bring about reform of French colonial policy in Africa. In 1947 he was awarded the Nobel Prize in Literature.

Gillespie, Dizzie 1917–93, American jazz musician and composer. Born in Cheraw, South Carolina, Gillespie learned to play the trumpet from his father, and studied theory at Laurinberg Institute. He played with the bands of Cab Calloway, Earl Hines, Villy Eckstein, and others. In the 1940s Gillespie, along with Charlie Parker and others, created bebop, a new style that transformed jazz.

Goethe, Johann Wolfgang von (1749-1832). German poet. Born in Frankfurt, Goethe was a law student in Leipzig and Strasbourg when he became interested in the arts and began writing poetry and plays. He came to love German folksong and Shakespearean drama, and used them as sources of inspiration for his work. He was a central figure in the German literary movement known as *Sturm und Drang,* which rejected classicism in favor of emotion, subjectivity, rebellion, and creative spontaneity. *The Sorrows of Young Werther,* a novel based on Goethe's own experience of unrequited love, made him famous throughout Europe. He became a leader of cultural life in Weimar, at that time the literary and intellectual center of Germany. There he also served in important governmental positions. Goethe was also a scientist, and made discoveries in biological morphology and optics. A gifted musician, fluent in many tongues, he was astounding for the range of his achievements. Goethe is a great figure in world literature. His masterpiece is the dramatic poem *Faust,* a reworking of a traditional legend into a philosophic treatment of the human quest for knowledge.

Goodman, Roy M. (1930-). American politician. Born in New York City, Goodman has served in the New York State Senate since 1966.

Gordon, Ruth (1896-1985). American actress and playwright. Born in Wollaston, Massachusetts, Ruth Gordon made her acting debut in a 1915 production of *Peter Pan*. She has written plays and screenplays, and won an Academy Award for her performance in the 1968 film *Rosemary's Baby*.

Grass, Günter (1927-). German writer. Born in Danzig, Germany (now Gdansk, Poland), Grass won international fame with his 1959 novel *The Tin Drum*. Grass's novels and plays employ black humor and an element of the bizarre, as well as brilliant use of language, to explore German history and politics. Grass won the 1999 Nobel Prize in Literature.

Grellet, Stephen (1773-1855). French Quaker missionary. The son of well-to-do Catholic parents, Grellet fled the French Revolution, settling in the United States in 1795. There, he became a Quaker, and eventually a minister. His profits from trade in New York City funded missionary expeditions all across the United States, Canada, and Europe. Everywhere he traveled, he investigated social conditions, and issues such as poverty and education, meeting with leaders and making recommendations based on his findings.

Gretzky, Wayne (1961-). Canadian ice hockey player. Born in Brantford, Ontario, Gretzky showed his talent on the ice early on, attracting crowds of fans as an amateur player by the time he was 16. In 1979 he joined the National Hockey League. Some felt that Gretzky, slight in size, would be overwhelmed by the bruising physical play of the NHL. Instead, Gretzky revolutionized ice hockey with his skill and speed. In 1988, Gretzky was traded to the Los Angeles Kings, saddening Canadians, but boosting the popularity of ice hockey in the U.S. He retired in 1999, having achieved 61 NHL records.

Hall, Monty (1923-). American quiz show host. Born in Winnipeg, Canada, Monty Hall served as emcee of Canadian Army shows during World War II. In the 50s, he came to New York to work in television. Hall is best known as the host and co-creator of the television quiz show *Let's Make a Deal*, which ran from 1963 to 1986. He is active in many charities.

Hamilton, Edith (1867-1963). American classical scholar. Born in Dresden, Germany, Hamilton was introduced to classical studies by her father. She pursued graduate study in Latin and Greek at Bryn Mawr College in Pennsylvania and at the Universities of Leipzig and Munich in Germany. After serving as the headmistress of a Baltimore school, Hamilton devoted herself to scholarship. The author of works including *The Roman Way* and *The Echo of Greece*, she was in 1957 elected to the American Academy of Arts and Letters and made an honorary citizen of Athens, Greece.

Hammerstein, Oscar II (1895-1960). American librettist. Born in New York City, Hammerstein achieved fame for his collaborations with Richard Rodgers on such acclaimed musicals as *Oklahoma!* and *South Pacific*.

Harburg, E.Y. (1896-1981). American lyricist. Born in New York City, Edgar "Yip" Harburg decided to be a lyricist when he heard Gilbert and Sullivan's *H.M.S. Pinafore*. He initially supported himself selling electrical appliances; his lyrics were performed for the first time on Broadway in 1926. In the years that followed he penned such standards as 'Brother, Can You Spare a Dime?' and 'Over the Rainbow'. In 1947 he was blacklisted in Hollywood for his political beliefs, so he returned to Broadway, where he worked until 1977.

Hare, J. C. (1795-1855). British cleric, writer. Julius Charles Hare wrote theological works. *Guesses at Truth*, written in 1847 in collaboration with his brother, the cleric Augustus Hare, was his most widely read book.

Hawking, Stephen (1942-). English physicist. Born in Oxford, England, Hawking was educated at Oxford and Cambridge. Hawking continued to teach and research even after a muscular disease, diagnosed in 1962, confined him to a wheelchair and made him dependent on a computer-generated voice synthesizer to communicate. In 1971, Hawking provided mathematical support for the big-bang theory of the universe. He made several important discoveries about the properties of black holes. His propositions mathematically linked gravity, quantum mechanics, and thermodynamics for the first time. In 1981, he proposed that the universe has no boundary, but is finite in space-time. His 1988 bestseller *A Brief History of Time: From the Big Bang to Black Holes* explains his work for a general audience.

Haywood, John (c.1497-c.1580). English dramatist. A court musician and playwright, Haywood was the author of ballads, epigrams, and proverbs. He was famous for short comic dialogues such as *The Play of the Weather*. A Catholic, he fled England for Belgium when Elizabeth I became queen.

Hazlitt, William (1778-1830). English writer. Hazlitt studied painting, but in 1805 gave it up in favor of writing. He wrote for newspapers as a reporter and as a theatre critic, and became a popular lecturer. His essays, which comprehended literary criticism, autobiography, and politics, are collected in volumes such as *Table Talk* and *The Plain Speaker*.

Hemingway, Ernest (1899–1961). American writer. Born in Oak Park, Illinois, Hemingway was an ambulance driver in World War I and later, a newspaper correspondent in Paris. There he became part of a circle of expatriate artists and writers surrounding Gertrude Stein, a writer whose influence can be seen in Hemingway's terse, often monotonous prose style. His 1926 novel *The Sun Also Rises*, about disillusioned expatriates in postwar Paris, won him recognition as the spokesman of "the lost generation" of the 1920s. His experiences during the war also became the basis for a novel, 1929's *A Farewell to Arms*. His great 1940 novel *For Whom the Bell Tolls* is set in the Spanish Civil War, in which Hemingway served as a correspondent on the republican side. He also fought in World War II. In 1945 he went to live in Cuba, but was expelled by Fidel Castro. From then on he lived in Idaho. In 1954, Hemingway was awarded the Nobel Prize for Literature. Hemmingway's work celebrates virility, courage, and the primal, elemental side of life. His pared-down, powerfully simple language was well suited to his themes, and had a great influence on the writers that came after him.

Henry, O. (1862-1910). American writer. Born William Sydney Porter, O. Henry grew up in Greensboro, North Carolina. He left school at 15 to work in his uncle's drugstore. In his 20s, he moved to Texas, and worked as a clerk and a bank teller. In his 30s, he began to write for newspapers. He first began to write short stories while in prison on charges of embezzlement, which may or may not have been true. After his release, he moved to New York City and wrote prolifically, becoming one of the most popular writers in America. His simple stories, with their use of ironic coincidence and surprise endings, have influenced short fiction, television, and film. O. Henry is also notable for the way he captures the rhythms of New York street life.

Hepburn, Katharine (1907-). American actress. Born in Hartford, Connecticut, Hepburn was the daughter of a doctor and a suffragette. She was encouraged in her athleticism and independence by her parents. After her brother's accidental death at 14, Hepburn became shy and withdrawn, and was schooled at home. However, she attended Bryn Mawr College, and began acting in plays there. After graduation, she began appearing on Broadway, and then in films. Despite the huge popularity of movies such as *Little Women,* Hepburn won the enmity of critics and audiences for her refusal to play the role of a Hollywood star. Hepburn wore slacks and no makeup; she did not pose for photographs or give interviews. Her independence was condemned as arrogance, and her films began to flop. Hepburn then went back to Broadway, and after the success of *The Philadelphia Story,* which also was adapted to the screen, she once again won the admiration of audiences. Hepburn has won four Academy awards.

Heraclitus, (c.535–c.475 B.C.) Greek philosopher. Born in Epheseus, a Greek city in Asia Minor (today Turkey), Heraclitus lived a solitary life. He taught that all things carry their opposite within them. He believed that permanence is an illusion; reality exists in a state of flux. Everything in the world is in a constant state of "becoming". He took fire to be the primordial source of life, because it is in a constant state of change.

Herodotus (c.484–c.425 B.C.) Greek historian. Born in Halicarnassus, Asia Minor, Herodotus traveled throughout Asia Minor, Babylonia, Egypt, and Greece. He used this knowledge of the world, as well as accounts of earlier writers, to write his classic *History.* It was the first work of its kind; Herodotus is called the father of history.

Herold, Don (1889-1966). American advertising executive. Herold was the author of *Humor in Advertising, and How to Make it Pay,* as well as several books of humor and illustrations.

Hesburgh, Theodore (1917-). American priest. Born in Syracuse, New York, Hesburgh knew as a young child that he wanted to be a priest.

He was ordained in 1943. In 1945, he joined the religion department of Notre Dame University, and rose to become university president in 1952. In his 35 years as president, Hesbergh worked to transform Notre Dame into a great university. He became a figure of national importance, serving on the U.S. Civil Rights Commission and in other public roles.

Hitchcock, Alfred (1899–1980). English-American filmmaker. Born in London, Hitchcock began his filmmaking career in 1919 illustrating title cards for silent films. He directed his first film in 1925, and in 1940 he began working in the United States. A master of suspense, Hitchcock virtually invented the thriller genre. In classic films such as *39 Steps, Strangers on a Train,* and *Notorious,* Hitchcock explored the darker side of the human psyche within the framework of a suspenseful story. He was knighted in 1980.

Hoffer, Eric (1902–1983). American philosopher. Born in New York City, Hoffer was the son of German-Jewish immigrants. When he was seven, Hoffer's mother died, and he went blind. He never had any formal education. At age 15, he regained his sight, and began to read avidly. When his father died two years later, Hoffer, without money and without skills, moved to Los Angeles. He worked at a variety of menial jobs, and spent the rest of his time in the public library, reading and writing. In 1942, he began a 25-year career as a longshoreman in San Francisco. His first book, *The True Believer,* a work on the origins of mass movements, was published in 1951. Hoffer held a prominent and controversial position in political thought for the ensuing forty years.

Holmes, Oliver Wendell, Jr. (1841-1935). American jurist. Born in Boston, Holmes served with distinction in the Civil War. He became a lawyer, achieving international renown for his lectures on the origin and nature of law, collected in *The Common Law.* He served 20 years in the Massachusetts Supreme Court, and from 1902 to 1932 served in the U.S. Supreme Court. Called the Great Dissenter for his disagreements with his fellow Justices and for his eloquently written opinions, Holmes defended the First Amendment and judicial restraint. He is remembered for his learning, wit, sound judgment, and eloquence.

Hopper, Edward (1882-1967). American painter. Born in Nyack, New York, Hopper spent his early years studying in New York City and visiting Europe. His paintings did not initially attract much interest, and he supported himself as an illustrator until he was over 40. In

1924 he married a fellow painter. The couple lived a simple, frugal life, devoted to painting. They spent winters in an old house in New York City's Washington Square, and summers in New England; these places were the subject of the majority of Hopper's paintings. Suffused in a mood of melancholy and loneliness, Hopper's spare, geometric paintings nonetheless have a poignant loveliness. They depict 20th century America with both poetry and realism.

Howe, Edgar Watson (1853-1937). American editor and author. Born in Treaty, Indiana, Howe was editor of a small town Kansas newspaper, the Atchison *Daily Globe*, and later founded *E.W. Howe's Monthly*. Howe, nicknamed the "Sage of Potato Hill," was known as a champion of the common man. He was the author of several novels, beginning in 1883 with *The Story of a Country Town*, which explores small-town life in the Midwest.

Hubbard, Elbert (1856–1915). American author and publisher. Born in Bloomington, Illinois, Hubbard founded an artist colony and a printing press, which produced fine books in the spirit of William Morris and the Arts and Crafts movement. Editor of *Philistine* magazine, Hubbard in 1899 wrote a famous inspirational essay on duty, "A Message to Garcia".

Hubbard, Kin (1868-1930). American humorist. Born Frank McKinney Hubbard in Bellefontaine, Ohio, Hubbard spent most of his life working as a newspaper artist in Indianapolis, Indiana. He won national fame for his cartoons featuring Abe Martin, a wise-cracking character from the Indiana backwoods who made pithy, humorous comments on politics and life.

Hugo, Victor (1802-85). French writer. Hugo began writing poetry at an early age, and soon joined Romantic literary circles. He became one of the most important figures in Romanticism. His poetry, plays, and novels often expressed his belief in freedom and his increasingly liberal politics. Following the Revolution of 1848, he served in the Legislative Assembly. When Napoleon III took power, Hugo was forced into exile. He produced some of his best work while in exile, completing his immensely popular novel *Les Miserables,* and *Les Contemplations,* a volume of moving poems reflecting on his daughter's tragic death. With the proclamation of the Third Republic, Hugo returned to France in triumph. In his last years he was venerated as a writer and a symbol of republicanism.

Hurston, Zora Neale (1891-1960). American writer. Hurtson was born and raised in Eatonville, Florida, the first black township to be incorporated in the United States. At Howard University she met Alain Locke who encouraged her writing and paved the way for her move to New York. Hurtson would become a major figure of the Harlem Renaissance, writing such classics as *Their Eyes Were Watching God* and *Of Mules and Men.* Despite her notoriety, Hurston slipped into near anonymity by the 1950s, working as a cleaning woman in Florida and dying in 1960. Her grave went unmarked until 1973 when novelist Alice Walker had a tombstone erected in the approximate area of her gravesite.

Huxley, Aldous (1894–1963). English author. Educated at Eton and Oxford, Huxley traveled widely and during the 1920s lived in Italy. He moved to California in the 1930s. Nearly blind since the age of eighteen, Huxley spent a great deal of time and energy attempting to improve his vision. His novels, which include *Point Counter Point, Brave New World,* and *Eyeless in Gaza* are inventive, sharply satirical depictions of modern society. His later writings reveal a bent towards mysticism and Eastern philosophy.

Iacocca, Lee (1924-). American executive. Born Lido Anthony Iacocca in Allentown, Pa., Iacocca joined the Ford Motor Company in 1946, and became president in 1970. In 1978 he left Ford and joined the failing Chrysler Corporation. As president and then chairman of Chrysler, Iacocca turned the company around through layoffs, cutbacks, advertising, and a government loan guarantee and tax concessions. His 1984 autobiography, *Iacocca,* was a best-seller.

Ignatius of Loyola, Saint. (1491-1556). Spanish founder of the Jesuits. Born to a noble family, Ignatius left court for the army. He resolved on a religious life while convalescing from a serious wound. He and his followers founded the Society of Jesus in 1539. Ignatius' main aim for the Jesuits was the establishment of schools and foreign missions. Over a number of years, he wrote *Spiritual Exercises,* a book of reflections and prayers that is a classic of Catholic mysticism. The spirituality of St. Ignatius emphasized human endeavor and spiritual direction.

Inge, William Ralph (1913–73). American playwright. Born and raised in Kansas, Inge wrote plays about the desires and frustrations of people in the small towns of the Midwest.

Itzhak Perlman 1(945-). Israeli-American violinist. A child prodigy, Perlman came to New York at the age of 13 and studied at the Juilliard School. He is one of the world's greatest violinists. Crippled by polio when he was four, Perlman has also been an advocate for the rights of the disabled.

Jackson, Andrew (1767–1845). United States president. Born in the backwoods of the Carolinas and orphaned at 14, Jackson rose to become a prosperous lawyer, a planter, and Tennessee's first Representative in the U.S. Congress. Then the war of 1812 erupted, and Jackson defeated the British in the Battle of New Orleans. Popular as a war hero and perceived as a champion of the majority rather than the elite, he was elected president in 1828. Jackson concentrated power in the office of the presidency. Taking what was for his period an advanced position on civil equality, and seen by many as a symbol of the democratic feelings of the time, he was an important founder of the ideology of the Democratic Party. Ferocious with those he saw as enemies, Jackson was kind with women and children, and was known for his magnetic personality.

James, Henry (1843–1916). American author. Born in New York City, James was educated by private tutors in New York, London, Paris, and Geneva. In his early 20s James began writing fiction and criticism for the magazine *The Atlantic Monthly*. In 1875, he settled permanently in London. James was a prolific writer of novels, short stories, plays, literary criticism, and travel essays. In novels such as *Portrait of a Lady* James portrays the contrast between American and European cultures as a contrast between innocence and experience. James presents his complex characters with a detachment and cool analysis befitting an expatriate, and in an intricate prose style distinctively and elegantly his own.

James, William (1842-1910). American psychologist and philosopher. The brother of the novelist Henry James, William James was brought up in an intellectual, cosmopolitan home. He grew up debating philosophical and religious principles with his father, a follower of the theology of Emmanuel Swedenbourg. As a young man, he was plagued by ill health, phobias and melancholy. He reached a personal and intellectual turning-point when, in his study of philosophy, he embraced free will and rejected scientific, theological, and metaphysical determinisms. Later, as a teacher of physiology at Harvard, William James, an M.D., challenged the dominant religious approach to psychology, and established a scientific approach. His 1890 work *Principles of Psychology* revolutionized the field. James then turned to religious questions, writing books such as the classic *Varieties of Religious Experience*. Finally, James addressed problems of philosophy. His philosophy of pragmatism revitalized the discipline in the English-speaking world.

Jefferson, Thomas (1743-1826). Jefferson was a leader of the patriot faction in Virginia's colonial House of Burgesses. He was a delegate to the Second Continental Congress, and was the author of the Declaration of Independence. In the Virginia legislature, Jefferson worked towards establishing religious freedom, and worked against aristocracy by abolishing primogeniture and entail. He was governor of Virginia during the final years of the American Revolution. He served as U.S Minister to France from 1785 to 1789, and became America's first Secretary of State upon his return. Seeing a threat to agrarian interests and democratic values in Federalist policies and ideology, Jefferson became the leader of Anti-Federalist party, the Democratic Republicans, to which the present-day Democratic party traces its origins. Antagonism with the leader of the Federalists, Treasury Secretary Alexander Hamilton, led Jefferson to leave the cabinet. The Republicans triumphed in 1800, and Jefferson became president. As president, he advocated a limited role for the federal government, strictly defined by the constitution, allowing the states to play a broader role. Despite some qualms about its constitutionality, he pushed through the Louisiana Purchase. In his second administration, Jefferson attempted to respond to attacks on American shipping by warring Britain and France with an unpopular trade embargo. After he left office, he lived in retirement at Monticello, his beloved estate. He was the founder and architect of the University of Virginia. Jefferson's eloquent writings remain a touchstone of the democratic ideals. He is an inspirational symbol for both American political parties, and to people around the world.

Jesus Christ (c.6 B.C.-c.30 A.D.). Jesus was born in Bethlehem and raised in Nazareth by his mother, Mary, and her husband, a carpenter. As a young man, he followed the carpenter's trade. After being baptized in the Jordan River by John the Baptist, Jesus began his public ministry, healing the sick, teaching moral lessons through parables, and spreading the message of God's love. Jesus was beloved by the populace; his followers believe he is the Son of God. The religious and political authorities had him executed. According to the Gospels, he rose from the dead, and appeared to his disciples, before finally rising to heaven. Christianity is based on his life and teachings.

Jiménez, Juan Ramón (1881-1958). Spanish poet. Born in Andalusia, Jiménez left Spain during the civil war and taught literature in the United States, Cuba, and Puerto Rico. Influenced by French symbolism and Spanish modernism, Jiménez's poems employ subtle nuances of rhythm and tone. They often deal with melancholy and suffering. Jiménez's works include *Spiritual Sonnets* and *Diary of a Newly Married Poet*. He won the Nobel Prize in 1956.

Joel, Billy (1949-). American musician. Born in the Bronx, New York, Joel began taking piano lessons at age four, and played in numerous bands in high school. Joel played in piano lounges until "Piano Man", a song he wrote about that experience, became a hit in 1973. Many more hits followed. Recently, Joel has been composing music in a classical vein.

John XXIII, Pope (1881-1963). Italian pope. Born Angelo Giuseppe Roncalli near Bergamo, Italy, he was ordained in 1904. He became pope in 1958. As pope, he promoted social reform to benefit workers, the poor, the outcast, and assistance to underdeveloped countries. The major accomplishment of his reign was convening the Second Vatican Council, with the goal of the spiritual renewal of the church and the reconsideration of its role in the modern world. Pope John XXIII 's receptivity to church reform, as well as his openness to other faiths and his optimistic, hearty, caring nature, made him one of the most beloved popes of modern times.

Johnson, Lady Bird (1912–). Born Claudia Alta Taylor in Karnack, Texas, Lady Bird married Lyndon B. Johnson in 1934. She played an active role in his political career. As first lady she sponsored highway beautification. She was also a successful businesswoman and rancher.

Johnson, Lyndon B. (1908-73). Born into a farm family near Stonewall, Texas, Johnson began his political career as secretary to a Texas Congressman. An enthusiastic New Dealer, Johnson was appointed Texas administrator for the National Youth Administration in 1935. Two years later he was elected to Congress. He served in the Navy during World War II. In 1948 he was elected to the Senate, where he rose rapidly to become Democratic whip and floor leader. When he lost the Democratic nomination for president in 1960, he joined John F.

Kennedy's ticket. When Johnson became president after Kennedy's assassination, he got Congress to pass a sweeping civil-rights bill, a voting rights bill, a Medicare bill, and education and environmental legislation. Johnson's vision of a "Great Society", however, was tarnished by problems abroad. As Johnson authorized bombing and deployed hundreds of thousands of American troops in Vietnam, the rising war costs led Congress to abandon many of his domestic programs. Opposition to Johnson's actions in Vietnam was widespread among the public and in Congress. Johnson decided not to run for reelection in 1968.

Johnson, Samuel (1709-84). English writer. The son of a bookseller, Johnson was a brilliant student. He had to leave Oxford after his first year because of lack of funds. Johnson's work includes literary criticism, biographies, poems, and essays on politics and on the concerns of daily life, and a groundbreaking dictionary. This varied work, even including the dictionary, is full of eloquence, wit and also a high seriousness. Johnson was famous for his dazzling conversation, and had many friends in literary and artistic circles. Johnson suffered from poverty for much of his life, and from illness that was not only painful but disfiguring. He overcame these severe obstacles to become one of the greatest figures of eighteenth century life and letters.

Johnson, William H. (1901-70). American painter. As a young boy in rural North Carolina, Johnson frequently copied comic strips between working at odd jobs to help support his family. He came to New York at 17, intending to become a newspaper cartoonist. He studied painting at New York's National Academy of Design and in Paris. Like other black artists of the 20s and 30s, he lived in Europe for many years, where he found less racism and greater opportunities as an artist. Influenced by European painters such as Chaim Soutine and Oskar Kokoschka, Johnson developed an expressionist style of painting. Johnson returned to New York on the eve of World War II, where he taught at the Harlem Community Art Center. His return to New York, as well as trips to his hometown of Florence, North Carolina, inspired him to take up African-American subjects. He began painting works like 1940's *Farm Couple at Work*, the colorful, direct depictions of black rural and urban life for which he is best known. Johnson's mature style, most visibly influenced by folk art, also had roots in his study of African sculpture and in the painterly language of European modernism.

Joplin, Janice (1943-70). Born in Port Arthur, Texas, Joplin began singing in the country western clubs of Austin and Houston when she was 18. In 1963 she hitchhiked to California, and became part of the counterculture, singing blues in San Francisco and Venice Beach. She became the vocalist for Big Brother and the Holding Company, a rock band. Joplin's fierce blues sound attracted attention; their 1968 album *Cheap Thrills* went to the top of the charts. That same year, Joplin left the group in order to pursue a solo career. She gave a memorable performance at the Woodstock festival in 1969. In 1970, she died of a heroin overdose. The emotion and power of Joplin's singing, and the passion and disillusionment she sang about, made her an icon of her generation.

Jordan, David Starr (1851–1931). American scientist, educator, and peace activist. Born in Gainesville, New York, Jordan was a leading ichthyologist who served on international commissions for fisheries and as assistant to the U.S. Fish Commission. He also served as president of Indiana University and Stanford University, as director of the World Peace Foundation, and of the World Peace Congress, campaigning vigorously against American involvement in World War I. A popular speaker, Jordan also authored many books on ichthyology, on education, and on peace and international arbitration.

Joubert, Joseph (1754–1824). French moralist. Born in Montignac, France, Joubert became part of Paris literary and intellectual circles. The writer Chateaubriand had Joubert's *Pensées* privately printed in 1838. The elegant and incisive *Pensées* deal with ethics, politics, theology, and literature.

Jung, Carl (1875–1961). Swiss psychiatrist. Jung founded analytic psychology, and was president from 1911 to 1912 of the International Psychoanalytic Society. He developed a scheme to classify personalities into extroverted and introverted types, and mental functions into thinking, feeling, sensation and intuition. He developed the theory of a collective unconscious and archetypes. For Jung, a person's task in life is fulfillment through the process of individuation, and achievement of harmony of conscious and unconscious, which makes a person whole.

Kaiser, Henry J. (1882-1967). American industrialist. Born in Sprout Brook, New York, Kaiser became a leader in highway construction. In 1931 he directed the construction of the Hoover Dam. He directed the production of ships, planes, and military vehicles during World War II. After the war, he founded several corporations including Kaiser Steel.

Keller, Helen (1880-1968). American author and lecturer. Born in Alabama, Keller suffered an illness at the age of 19 months, leaving her blind and deaf. When she was seven years old, Anne Sullivan Macy of the Perkins Institute for the Blind became her teacher, and Keller learned how to read, write, and speak. Keller eventually attended Radcliffe College, graduating with honors in 1904. Throughout her life, Keller traveled the world lecturing on behalf of the blind. Her books include *The Story of My Life* and *The Open Door*.

Kennedy, John F. (1917-63). United States president. Kennedy was born in Brookline, Massachusetts, to a wealthy, politically active family. He won a medal for courage while serving in the Navy during World War II. When his brother Joe, who had planned on a political career, was killed in 1944, John F. Kennedy decided to enter politics. He became a congressman in 1947, a senator in 1952, and in 1960 was elected president. Kennedy embarked on a domestic program called the New Frontier. Congress passed his legislation to accelerate the space program, increase the minimum wage, grant federal aid to economically depressed areas, and create the Peace Corps. Later on in his administration, Kennedy found it difficult to get his programs, such as the Medicare bill and a civil rights bill, passed. The first of several foreign affairs crises came in 1961 with the failure of the U.S.-orchestrated Bay of Pigs invasion of Cuba. Several months later, a meeting between Kennedy and Khruschev, the Soviet premier, revealed an increase in Cold War hostility; the Berlin Wall was built shortly thereafter. In 1962, the Americans discovered Soviet missile bases in Cuba; Kennedy demanded their removal, and after a period of extreme tension, the Soviets complied. Kennedy was praised by many for his firm stance, which may have prevented a nuclear war. Assassinated after less than three years in office, Kennedy was deeply mourned by the nation. The youngest president in U.S. history, and the first to be born in the 20th century, he represented to many a new spirit in Washington and in the country.

Kennedy, Robert F. (1925-1968). American politician. After serving in the Navy during World War II, Kennedy graduated from Harvard and the University of Virginia Law School. He managed his brother John's successful Senate campaign in 1952. He then served as counsel to several Senate subcommittees, first gaining national prominence for exposing corruption in the Teamsters Union. In 1960, he managed his brother's presidential campaign, and was appointed to his cabinet. As attorney general, he prosecuted civil rights cases with vigor. In 1964 he was elected U.S. senator from New York. In the Senate, Kennedy was an advocate for minorities and the poor, and fought for social reform. Kennedy was campaigning for the Democratic nomination in the 1968 presidential race when he was shot dead in Los Angeles.

Kennedy, Rose Fitzgerald (1890-1995). American author and philanthropist. The daughter of Boston mayor John F. "Honey Fitz" Fitzgerald, Rose Fitzgerald married businessman Joseph P. Kennedy. She raised nine children. While she saw many of them go on to high achievements, she also had to endure the tragedy of the violent deaths of four of her children. She is the author of *Times to Remember*.

Kierkegaard, Søren (1813-55). Danish philosopher. Soren Kierkegaard was born in Copenhagen. His father was a wealthy man, who had risen from humble beginnings in the desolate moors of western Jutland. While a young tenant farmer, he had stood on a hill and solemnly cursed God, out of poverty and despair. Søren Kierkegaard inherited his father's melancholy and guilt, and his fear that the family might be cursed by God. Kierkegaard studied theology and philosophy, and lived a life of intense inner examination and reflection on the human condition. He broke off an engagement with a girl he loved because, weighed down by a sense of guilt and an acute awareness of human complexity, he felt unable to connect with someone young and innocent. This painful decision provided material for *Either/Or* and *Stages on Life's Way*, works that compares ethical, religious and aesthetic approaches to life. Kierkegaard emphasized free will, responsibility, and the importance of choosing among life's alternatives. He is regarded as the founder of existentialist philosophy.

Killebrew, Harmon (1936-). American baseball player. Born in Payette, Idaho, Harmon Killebrew began his major-league career in 1954, with the Washington Senators, later the Minnesota Twins. He became one of the best hitters in baseball. In 1969 he won both the American League's Most Valuable Player Award and the Sporting News's Player-of-the-Year Award. He retired in 1975, and turned to sports broadcasting.

King, Martin Luther, Jr. (1929-68). American clergyman and civil rights leader. The son of a Baptist minister in Atlanta, Georgia, Dr. Martin

Luther King, Jr. became a minister of a Baptist church in Montgomery, Alabama. In 1955, he led the boycott of the segregated city bus lines by Montogomery blacks. After the success of this campaign in 1956, King helped found the Southern Christian Leadership Conference (SCLC), an organization of black clergyman and churches working to end segregation. King and the SCLC led a series of nonviolent protest campaigns that gained national attention. When a protest march was met by police violence in Birmingham, Alabama, pictures of nonviolent marchers attacked by police dogs shocked the world. Arrested during the march, King wrote his famous "Letter from Birmingham Jail" explaining his conviction in the individual's moral duty to disobey unjust laws. He was one of the leaders of the 1963 March on Washington, where he gave his famous and moving "I Have a Dream" speech to an audience of 200,000 civil rights supporters. In 1964, the Civil Rights Act was passed, ending segregation and prohibiting racial discrimination. The same year King won the Nobel Peace Prize. In the second half of the 1960s, King campaigned against poverty and the Vietnam war. Assassinated in 1968, King has become a powerful symbol of racial justice and moral leadership for Americans.

Kingsley, Charles (1819–75). English author and clergyman. The son of a Devon vicar, Charles Kingsley became curate of Eversley in Hampshire in 1842. In 1848, he helped form the Christian Socialist movement. Kingsley published articles in Christian Socialist journals. In novels such as *Alton Locke* Kingsley attempts to expose social injustice. In 1859, Kingsley was made chaplain to Queen Victoria. From 1860 to 1869 he was professor of modern history at Cambridge and in 1873 was appointed canon of Westminster. His work includes the children's classic *The Water Babies*.

Kipling, Rudyard (1865-1936). English writer. Born in Bombay, India, Kipling was sent to England at age six. From 1882 to 1889 he was a writer and editor for the *Civil and Military Gazette* of Lahore, India. In 1888 he began publishing the short stories about life in colonial India that made him famous. After extensive traveling, he settled in England in 1903. He wrote stories and verse prolifically, attaining wide popularity. His writing usually conveys a patriotic message of British duty and destiny. Nonetheless, it also displays extensive knowledge of and affection for India. Perhaps his best work is his collection of animal stories, *The Jungle Book*. He won the Nobel Prize in 1907.

Klotsche, J. Martin (1907-1995). American educator. Klotsche was professor of history and president of Milwaukee State Teachers College-Wisconsin State College from 1946 to 1956, and provost-chancellor of University of Wisconsin at Milwaukee from 1956 to 1973. His books on higher education include *The Urban University and the Future of Our Cities.*

Kozol, Jonathan (1936-). Born in Boston, Kozol was a Rhodes scholar and a fiction writer with no involvement in social or political issues until 1964, when inspired by the civil rights movement, he took a job as a teacher in an impoverished, black Boston neighborhood. Based on this experience, he wrote *Death at an Early Age: The Destruction of the Hearts and Minds of Negro Children in the Boston Public Schools,* which served to draw national attention to the tremendous problems in inner-city schools. Kozol has continued to investigate and write about the plight of poor people, in particular black children in urban ghettos.

La Rochefoucauld, François, Duc de (1613-80). French moralist. Born in Paris, La Rouchefoucauld was a prominent in court and political life. His famous *Reflections or Moral Thoughts and Maxims* are a collection of witty, pithy, and wise maxims.

Lamartine, Alphonse de (1790–1869). French poet. After a trip to Italy and a brief period in the army, Lamartine began to write and achieved immediate success with his first publication, *Méditations poétiques* (1820). This group of poems expressed his feelings as he made contact with nature. Lamartine believed in democracy, social justice, and international peace. After the February Revolution of 1848 Lamartine participated in government. A moderate, he lost the support of both the right and the left wings of the revolutionists. He eventually devoted his life to writing and to paying the debts he had accumulated as a young man.

Lamb, Charles (1775–1834). English essayist. Born in London, Lamb went to school at Christ's Hospital, where he began a lifelong friendship with Coleridge. Lamb worked as a clerk from 1792 to 1825. In 1796 his sister Mary Ann Lamb in a fit of temporary insanity attacked their parents, killing their mother. To save her from life in an asylum, Lamb became her guardian, and lived with her from 1799 onwards. Despite their affectionate relationship, the Lamb siblings were burdened by Mary's mental illness. They collaborated on several books for children, publishing in 1807 their famous *Tales from Shakespeare*. Lamb wrote four plays, none of which were successful. However, he achieved success as a critic with his 1808 work *Specimens of English Dramatic Poets*. His *Essays of Elia* embrace a variety of topics. Lamb's revealing observations on life, and his humor, fantasy, and pathos make him one of the great English essayists.

Lamb, Mary (1765-1847). English writer. In 1796, during a period of insanity, Mary Lamb killed her mother, but was spared life in an institution by her brother Charles, who made himself her guardian. They were excellent companions, as well as literary collaborators, but the tragedy and Mary's periods of mental illness continued to cast a shadow over their lives. Mary co-authored several works with her brother, including the children's book *Tales from Shakespeare*

Landers, Ann (1918-). American advice columnist. Born Esther Pauline Friedman, she began writing her column in 1955 under the name "Ann Landers." The column quickly became a success and is one of the most widely syndicated columns in the world. Landers has written five books and a number of pamphlets. Her twin sister, Pauline Esther, also writes an advice column, "Dear Abby."

Landor, Walter Savage (1775-1864). English writer. Although he quarreled with authorities and his family throughout his life, Landor had close friendships with many of the writers of his time. He wrote poems, plays, and essays. Landor is remembered for his *Imaginary Conversations,* nearly 150 dialogues between historical figures.

Lao-Tzu (c.570-c.490 B.C.). Chinese philosopher, reputed founder of Taoism. According to tradition, Lao-Tzu was a court librarian whose teachings were recorded in the *Tao-te Ching*. This work uses parables to describe the *Tao,* which is the way the universe functions and the path people must follow in order to be in harmony with the universe. It advocates contemplation and the renunciation of desire and striving. The *Tao-te Ching* has had a great influence on Chinese thought and culture, and in the last century has become popular in the West as well.

Lardner, Ring. (1885-1933). American writer and humorist. Born in Niles, Michigan, Lardner was a sports reporter for over a decade. *You Know Me, Al,* his first collection of short fiction, was the humorous account of the life of a baseball player. The author of many collections of short stories dealing with the lives of ordinary working people, he writes with a keen ear for speech and a deadpan sense of humor.

Lazarus, Emma (1849-1887). American poet and essayist. Born in New York City, Lazarus protested the Russian pogroms of the 1880s with essays and her 1882 poetry collection *Songs of a Semite*. Her faith in the United States is expressed in her sonnet "the New Colossus", which is engraved on the pedestal of the Statue of Liberty.

Lennon, John (1940-80). English musician. Born in working-class Liverpool, Lennon started his first rock band, the Quarryman, while attending the Quarry Bank Grammar School. In 1957, Paul McCartney and George Harrison joined the group, which after several name changes became the Beatles. Lennon attended Liverpool College of Art from 1957 to 1960. The Beatles were wildly popular throughout the 1960s, and remain legendary today. Lennon's songwriting has greatly influenced rock and pop music. In later years, Lennon and his second wife, the Japanese artist and musician Yoko Ono, recorded albums together and spoke out for world peace. Lennon was deeply mourned by people around the world when he was assassinated in 1980.

Leonardo da Vinci (1452-1519). Italian artist. The illegitimate son of a wealthy Florentine notary and a peasant woman, Leonardo received an excellent education and was apprenticed to a leading painter. In 1478 he became an independent artist, and in 1482 went to the court of the duke of Milan, where for 16 years he served as an artist, as an engineer, and as an architect. In 1802 he became a military engineer to Cesare Borgia, the duke of Romagna. He later served as court painter, architect, and engineer in Milan and in Rome. Leonardo's innovations were key to the development of Renaissance painting. In the astonishing range of his talents, Leonardo was the paradigm of the Renaissance genius: he was not only a great painter and draftsman, but also a masterful architect, and, as a scientist, anticipated many of the discoveries of modern times.

Lewis, C.S. (1898–1963). English author. Born in Belfast, Ireland, Clive Staples Lewis was a fellow and tutor of English at Oxford, from 1925 to 1954, and a professor of Medieval and Renaissance English at Cambridge from 1954 until his death. Noted as a literary scholar, and for his inventive expositions of Christian tenets, Lewis is the author of many works of literary criticism. Lewis is also the author of *The Screwtape Letters*, an ironic treatment of the theme of salvation, and the "Chronicles of Narnia," a series of fantasy novels containing elements of Christian allegory that have become a classic of children's literature.

Lin Yutang (1895-1976). Chinese-American writer and scholar. Born in China, Lin was educated there and at Harvard and Leipzig. He lived most of his life in the United States and wrote most of his many works in English. His books include novels, and translations of ancient Chinese texts, as well as *The Importance of Living*, a popular book in which Lin applies insights gained from his study of Chinese philosophy to daily life.

Lincoln, Abraham (1809–65). United States president. Born in a log cabin in backwoods Kentucky to a poor farmer, Lincoln received almost no formal schooling. In 1831 he settled in the frontier town of New Salem, Illinois, where he worked as mill manager, a postmaster, and at a variety of odd jobs, all the while working on his education and studying law. His neighbors liked and respected him for his capability and strength of character, as well as for his storytelling and physical strength. In 1834, Lincoln was elected to the state legislature as a Whig, and served four terms. Except for one term in Congress, Lincoln spent the next twenty years practicing law in Springfield, Illinois. In 1858 Lincoln ran for senator against Stephen A. Douglas. Though Lincoln lost the election, he attracted national attention in a series of debates in which he spoke eloquently for the Union. In 1860, Lincoln was elected president, with a minority of the popular vote. To the South, Lincoln's election was the signal for secession, and the Civil War began. In the face of enormous challenges, Lincoln conducted the war with skill and wisdom. He was to have no chance to implement his vision of Reconstruction, which was one of forgiveness and regeneration, because he was assassinated just after the war ended.

Lippman, Walter (1889–1974), American journalist. As a journalist and an editor of the *The New Republic,* Lippman became an influential political commentator, and an adviser to presidents. He played a key role in a post-World War I peace conference, and helped formulate Wilson's 14 Points. He supported Lyndon Johnson's domestic policies, but broke with him over Vietnam.

Locke, John (1632-1704). English philosopher. Locke studied and taught at Oxford. He became physician, friend, and advisor to the statesman Anthony Ashley Cooper, who became the 1st Earl of Shaftesbury. Locke also held several government positions, and spent four years in France, where he met French scientists and philosophers.

In his *Essay on Human Understanding* Locke examines how human beings know the world. He believed that humans do not possess innate knowledge; rather, when we are born our mind is a *tabula rasa* or blank slate, which will receive impressions from the world. In his *Two Treatises on Civil Government* Locke attacked absolute monarchy. He held that sovereignty resides with the people, and set forth ideas for a "civil government" which later shaped the United States Constitution. Locke was called the "philosopher of freedom".

Lonergan, Bernard (1904-85). Jesuit theologian and philosopher. Born in Buckingham, Quebec, Canada, Lonergan entered the Society of Jesus in 1922, and was a professor of systematic theology at the Gregorian University in Rome. In works such as *Philosophy of God* and *Understanding and Being* he explored theology and the history of ideas.

Longfellow, Henry Wadsworth (1807-82). American poet. Born in Portland, Maine, Longfellow taught modern languages. Longfellow's long narrative poems such as *The Song of Hiawatha* created American legends. He was extremely popular during his lifetime, and helped create a public audience for poetry in America.

Louis, Joe (1914-1981). American boxer. The son of poor Alabama tenant farmers, Louis moved with his family to Detroit in 1926. Louis took up boxing, turning professional in 1934. Louis, with his physical superiority, quick combination punches, and calmness, defeated all comers, becoming heavyweight champion in 1937. Blacks had been kept out of major sports, and Louis's victories and fame made him a symbol of his race to both blacks and whites. In a time when blacks were kept out of all high positions, Louis was a source of hope and inspiration to many black people. Hitler had embraced German heavyweight Max Schmeling's 1936 victory over Louis as proof of Aryan superiority; two years later Louis knocked Schmeling out in the first round. Louis not only beat the only man who had ever beat him, he was hailed as a representative of American values triumphing over Nazism. Louis served in the army in the Second World War, and returned to defend his title twice before retiring in 1949.

Luckman, Charles (1809-1999) American businessman and architect. Born in Missouri, Luckman was educated as an architect. He first made a name for himself as a sales manager at Pepsodent. He became president of Lever at age 37. After commissioning Lever House, one of Manhattan's first glass skyscrapers, he returned to architecture. He designed Madison Square Garden and Florida's Kennedy Space Center.

Luther, Martin (1483-1546). Born in rural Saxony, Luther was studying law when a sudden religious experience impelled him to become an Augustinian friar. He devoted himself to observing the strict disciplines of his order and to studying Scripture. For years, Luther suffered spiritual torment, doubting his own salvation, which he assuaged with asceticism and further study. He drew from the Scriptures the message of God's love, and salvation through faith. He began to preach that salvation came through faith, as opposed to good works. In 1517 he famously nailed his 95 theses questioning the Church's dispensation of indulgences to a church door at Wittenburg. At this point Luther was still seeking reform within the Church, but he was seen as a heretic by his opponents. As debate continued, Luther's criticisms of the Church broadened. He attacked corruption, and denied the supremacy of the pope and other Church doctrines. His views garnered widespread popular support. After he was excommunicated, he spent some time in hiding from the authorities, but returned to Wittenburg to organize the new church. He married a former nun and had six children.

Lynd, Robert (1892-1970). American sociologist. Born in New Albany, Indiana, Lynd co-authored with his wife *Middletown: A Study in Contemporary American Culture*, a classic of American sociology. He also wrote *Knowledge for What?* which criticized sociology that emphasizes a quantitative or statistical approach.

Mack, Connie (1862-1956). American baseball owner. Originally a catcher, Mack gained fame as a manager. He assumed control of the Philadelphia Athletics in 1901 and continued for 50 years until retirement at the age of 88. He won five World Series crowns, and won four pennants in five years from 1910 to 1914 and three in a row from 1929 to 1931.

Mann, Horace (1796–1859). American educator. Despite an inadequate primary education, Mann managed to enter Brown University and graduate with honors in 1819. After serving in the Massachusetts state legislature, Mann became the Secretary of the State Board of Education. It was the first such board in the country, and during his 12 years of service Mann not only improved equipment, schoolhouses, and teacher training and pay in Massachusetts, he led public opinion in demanding change in other states. In 1843, Mann visited Europe to study their educational system. Back home his advocacy of certain European methods, such as the abolition of corporal punishment, brought controversy. Mann was elected to Congress in 1848, and in 1853 became the first president of Antioch College.

Mann, Thomas (1875-1955). German writer. Born in Lübeck, Germany, Mann lived in Munich from 1891 to 1933. He became famous with the 1901 publication of his first novel, *Buddenbrooks*, the story of the rise and disintegration of a bourgeois family. Mann's novels and essays often deal with the relationship between the artist and society, and between art and reality. During World War I, Mann wrote nationalistic, antidemocratic political essays. He attacked his brother Heinrich, also an author, and a critic of German authoritarianism. Later, Mann repudiated his position, and spoke out boldly against Nazism. His incredibly rich and nuanced novels, such as *The Magic Mountain*, present a deeper, more complex understanding of European politics and culture than his own political essays of the time, or the principled but propagandistic novels of his brother Heinrich. When Hitler became chancellor, Mann left Germany for Switzerland and the United States. He won the Nobel Prize in 1929.

Mansfield, Mike (1903-2001). U.S. Senator. Born in New York to Irish immigrant parents, Mansfield was sent to live with relatives in Montana at age three, following his mother's death. He served as a Navy seaman in World War I when he was 14 years old, and later served in the Army and the Marine Corps. At 19, he began working as a miner. At the urging of his future wife, Mansfield pursued a college education, graduating from Montana State University at Missoula in 1933 and receiving a Master's degree the next year. After eight years as a history professor, Mansfield was elected to Congress as a Democrat. He was elected to the Senate ten years later, and became majority whip in 1957. He held the post of Senate majority leader from 1961 to 1976, longer than anyone in Senate history. As a senator, Mansfield played a leading role in the 1964 Civil Rights Act, and was the leading congressional critic of the Vietnam war. He was a strong advocate of national health insurance. After retiring from the Senate, Mansfield served as American Ambassador to Japan.

Marcus Aurelius (121-180) Roman emperor. Marcus Aurelius succeeded his uncle Antoninus as emperor. He spent his reign defending the Roman empire against Parthians, Germans, and Britons.

He was a learned, conscientious, just, and humanitarian emperor, who sought to improve the conditions of the poor. His *Meditations* expresses his philosophy, which was based on Stoicism.

Martin Luther King, Sr. (1899-1984). American minister. Born Michael Luther King in Stockbridge, Georgia, King was the son of sharecroppers. Active in his church as a lay preacher and as a singer in gospel groups, King moved to Atlanta in 1918 with the goal of becoming a minister. He became pastor of two small community churches, where he was an energetic and popular preacher. He supported himself by working in the railroads, and attended night school. He received his high school diploma in 1925, and a B.A. in theology from Morehouse College in 1930. In 1931, he succeeded his father-in-law as pastor of the prestigious Ebenezer Baptist Church. Under his leadership, Ebenezer increased its membership from 600 to 4,000, and became Atlanta's leading Black church. As a leader in both religious and civil organizations, King fought for racial justice. His many civil rights activities included campaigns for voter's rights, integration of transportation, and equalizing black and white teachers' salaries. He continued to preach love and nonviolence even after the murders of his son, civil rights leader Martin Luther King, Jr., and of his wife.

Maugham, Somerset (1874-1965). English writer. Maugham was orphaned at 10, and brought up by an uncle. He became a doctor, but with the publication of his first novel, abandoned medicine for writing. He first made his reputation as a playwright, but is remembered today for his novels, particularly *Of Human Bondage*. This semi-autobiographical work relates a sensitive young doctor's painful progress to self-realization. Maugham's writings are characterized by wit and irony, and a clear style. Their cosmopolitan settings are drawn from Maugham's wide travels.

Maurice, Frederick Denison (1805-72). English clergyman and social reformer. Raised a Unitarian, Maurice refused to subscribe to the 39 Articles of the Church of England, costing him his Cambridge law degree. However, he later became a clergyman in the Church of England. After the 1853 publication of his *Theological Essays,* which questioned the concept of hell, he was forced to resign from his post as Professor of Divinity at Oxford. In 1848 he became one of the leaders of the Christian Socialist movement. A champion of education, Maurice founded the Working Men's College and Queen's College for women. He was a Professor of Moral Philosophy at Cambridge from 1866 until his death. He wrote one novel and many religious works.

Maxwell, William (1908-2000) American writer and editor. Born in Lincoln, Illinois, Maxwell was on the staff of the *New Yorker* magazine from 1936 to 1976. Maxwell's fiction includes the novel *The Folded Leaf,* which chronicles the friendship between two small-town boys. His novels and short stories are spare, evocative depictions of the small-town Midwest of his youth.

McLuhan, Marshall (1911-80). Canadian communications theorist. Born in Edmonton, Atlanta, McLuhan taught at universities in the United States and Canada, including the University of Toronto. He became famous in the 1960s for his insights into the transformations that television and other electronic media were effecting in contemporary culture. His books include *The Gutenburg Galaxy* and *The Mechanical Bride.*

Menninger, William (1899–1966). American psychiatrist. Dr. William Menninger founded the Menninger Clinic in Topeka, Kansas along with his father, Charles Fredrick, and his brother, Karl. The clinic was the first group psychiatry practice, and it reflected the Menningers' belief, advanced for the time, that people with mental illnesses could be treated and helped, not just kept in custodial care. Dr. William Menninger developed a system of hospital treatment known as milieu therapy, which involved a patient's total environment in treatment. During World War II he served as Chief of the Army Medical Corps' Psychiatric Division. After the war, he worked to reform state sanitariums.

Meyer, Alan H. (1922-). American advertising executive. Born in Peoria, Illinois, Meyer has been in advertising since 1955.

Millay, Edna St. Vincent (1892–1950). American poet. Raised in Maine by a poor, hardworking, and fiercely devoted single mother, Millay's poetry won her a scholarship to attend Vassar College. *Renascence,* her first book of poetry, appeared in 1917, the same year she graduated. She spent the next few years in the artistic milieu of New York City's Greenwich Village. Her charm and her bohemian lifestyle were as important as her fresh, lively verse in making her one of the most popular poets of her time.

Miller, Alice Duer (1874-1942). American writer. Alice Duer's wealthy and influential New York family lost their wealth in a banking crisis just after her debut into society. Duer wrote for magazines to pay her way through Barnard College, where she studied mathematics and astronomy. Later, she wrote light fiction. She also worked for women's suffrage, and wrote a newspaper column, "Are Women People?" In the 1920s she wrote screenplays for Hollywood.

Milton, John (1608-74). English poet. Born in London, Milton abandoned plans to enter the clergy in order to become a poet. After leaving Cambridge University, Milton retired to his father's country house and spent six years reading classics and history, and writing poetry. After settling in London, Milton became one of the ablest pamphleteers of his day. He wrote many tracts advocating the reform of the Church of England, freedom of the press, and other religious, social and political questions. He eventually served in the government of the Commonwealth. By 1652, he had completely lost his sight, and from then on relied on assistants. While writing prose and serving in the government, Milton composed his masterpiece, *Paradise Lost*, as well as sonnets that are considered among the best ever written. The epic poem *Paradise Lost* relates Satan's rebellion against God, and Adam and Eve's fall from the Garden of Eden. Milton declared his aim was to "justify the ways of God to men".

Molière (1622-1673). French playwright. Born Jean Baptiste Polquelin in Paris, Molière abandoned the secure position he could have inherited from his father, an upholsterer to the king's court, and became an actor and playwright. In 1658, after years of touring the provinces, Molière and his troupe were invited by Louis XIV to perform at the Palais Royal. His farces and comedies of manners were extremely popular, but their piercing satire brought on criticism. *Tartuffe*, which satirized religious hypocrisy, was banned from the stage through the efforts of the Church. However, the king always stood by him. Molière's plays were notable for their use of humor to explore complex moral and social issues, their sophisticated language, and their caricatures of vain, greedy, false, or tyrannical characters. Molière was France's greatest comic playwright; he has had tremendous influence on later theater.

Montaigne, Michel Eyquem de. (1533-1592). French essayist. Born near Bordeaux in southwest France, Montaigne received a classical education, served in the Bordeaux Parliament and the court of Charles

IX, and then retired to his country estate. There he wrote his *Essays*, establishing a new literary form – short, personal pieces on a wide range of subjects. The *Essays* reflect Montaigne's broad learning and Renaissance skepticism. At once autobiographical, philosophical, and practical, the *Essays* explore both Montaigne himself and a broad range of human experience. The son of a Catholic father and Protestant mother who had converted from Judaism, Montaigne believed in tolerance, moderation, and intellectual humility, and the need for intellectual self-examination.

Montesquieu, Charles de (1689–1755). French jurist and political philosopher. Montesquieu served in the parlement of Bordeaux and held a seat in the French Academy. He became famous as a writer with the 1721 appeareance of his *Persian Letters*. The *Letters*, supposedly the correspondence of Persian travelers in Europe, satirized French insititutions. His greatest work, *The Spirit of Laws*, is a study of different forms of government. Brilliantly written and extremely historically significant, it influenced the American Constitution.

Moore, George (1852–1933) Irish author. Born in Ireland, Moore studied art in Paris as a young man. Inspired by French realists such as Zola and Flaubert, Moore began to write novels such as *Esther Waters*, the story of a servant's life of hardship, whose naturalism challenged the conventions of the Victorian novel. In 1900 Moore returned to Ireland, where he founded the Abby Theatre and associated with Yeats and other writers of the Irish literary renaissance.

Morley, Christopher (1890–1957). American editor and author. Born in Haverford, Pennsylvania., Morely attended Haverford College and was a Rhodes scholar. He was one of the founders of the *Saturday Review of Literature*, of which he was an editor from 1924 to 1940. A prolific author, he wrote more than 50 books. His novels include *Parnassus on Wheels* and *The Haunted Bookshop*. He also revised *Bartlett's Familiar Quotations*.

Morley, John (1838-1923). English statesman and writer. Born in Blackburn, England, Morley was the editor of a liberal newspaper for 15 years. He was elected to Parliament in1883. As chief secretary for Ireland, Morley helped prepare the first and second Home Rule Bills, and as Secretary of State for India, sponsored reforms allowing some political role for Indians. When Britain entered World War I, Morley resigned from public life in protest. One of the best biographers of his time, he wrote lives of Voltaire, Cromwell, Gladstone, and others, as well as works on politics and literature.

Morris, William (1834-1896). English designer. While at Oxford, Morris was influenced by John Ruskin's writings on the social and moral basis of architecture, and by pre-Raphaelite artists' love for medieval art and craft. He founded a workshop, designing and producing furniture, wallpaper, textiles, stained glass, and other decorative arts. Morris's designs revolutionized English taste, which was at the time dominated by ornate Victorian design. His strong, simple forms were inspired by medieval crafts. Morris also employed fine craftsmanship, in conscious rejection of industrialism. As interested in social equality as in aesthetics, he sought to fight the alienation of the industrial worker by a return to the dignified labor of the craftsman. In his time, Morris was also a famous poet, although his poetry is not read today. In 1890, he founded the Kelmscott Press, which began a tradition of fine printing in England and America. Morris and the Arts and Crafts movement he began heralded a rise in the importance of design, and its linkage in the modern era with both art and social ideology.

Murray, W.H. (1913-96). British mountaineer and author. Murray began mountaineering in the Scottish Highlands in the 1930s. He first began to write about his experiences during World War II, while he was detained in prisoner of war camps in Germany, Italy, and Czechoslovakia. He was a member of the expedition that surveyed the route used to scale Mt. Everest for the first time. His writings include *The Story of Everest* and *Mountaineering in Scotland*.

Namath, Joe (1943-). American football player. Born in Beaver Falls, Pennsylvania, Namath was a star quarterback at the University of Alabama. In 1965 he signed on with the New York Jets, and quickly won many fans. Namath promised and delivered a Jets victory in the 1969 Super Bowl against the heavily favored Baltimore Colts. Namath retired in 1978, and continued to work as a television sports broadcaster, as well as acting in films and television.

Nevill, Dorothy (1826–1913). British hostess, horticulturalist, and writer. Lady Dorothy Nevill built 13 greenhouses in her 23-acre Hampshire garden, and amassed an important collection of plants. She corresponded with Darwin and other scientists. She was also noted as a society figure, a wit, and an author.

Newman, John Henry (1801–90). English churchman, Cardinal of the Roman Catholic Church. Born in London, Newman studied at Oxford, where he became tutor after his ordination in the Church of England. He was made vicar of St. Mary's, Oxford, in 1827. Newman became a leader of the Oxford movement, a movement to renew the Church of England by reviving certain Roman Catholic doctrines and rituals. In 1841 Newman published a highly controversial tract maintaining that the Thirty-nine Articles, the formulary of faith of the Church of England, were consistent with Catholicism. Newman eventually became a Catholic priest, and established the Congregation of the Oratory on the outskirts of Birmingham, where he remained for the rest of his life. Newman was created Cardinal in 1879 at the demand of English Catholics. Newman's essays are still popular today; his prose is lucid and convincing. His greatest work is his 1864 *Apologia pro vita sua*, a masterpiece of religious autobiography, which Newman wrote to refute Charles Kingsley's charge that the Catholic clergy was not interested in truth.

Nicole, Pierre (1625-95). French theologian. Nicole studied and taught at Port-Royal abbey, the center of Jansenism, the mystical Catholic movement. He sought to popularize Jansenism through his writings. He later became involved in other important theological controversies of his time.

Niebuhr, Reinhold (1892-1971). American religious and social thinker. As a pastor in Detroit, Niebuhr became deeply concerned with social issues. A political activist during the 1930s, and a professor at Union Theological Seminary, he influence American politcal and economic thought. Niebuhr advocated church interest in social reforms, and examined the interrelations between religion, man, and modern society. His many works include *Moral Man and Immoral Society* and *Faith and History.*

Nietzsche, Friedrich (1844-1900). German philosopher. Born in Röcken, Prussia, Nietzsche lost his father, a Lutheran minister, when he was five. He was brought up his mother, aunts, and grandmother. He was chair of classical philology at the University of Basel until eye problems and nervous ailments forced him to leave his job in 1879. He had a mental breakdown in 1889, and never recovered. Nietzsche's works, which include *The Birth of Tragedy, On the Geneology of Morals* and *The Will to Power* forcefully criticize traditional morality.

Nin, Anaïs (1903-77). American writer. Born in Paris to artistic parents, Nin and her family moved to New York in 1914. Largely self-educated, she spent her youth reading in public libraries and keeping a journal. In the 1930's Nin and her husband moved to France, where Nin began to write fiction. She fell in with the Villa Seurat Group, a circle of writers that included Henry Miller, with whom she had a passionate love affair. Nin was an early patient of Jung, and her work reflects a concern with the unconscious. The erotic is an important theme in her work. Nin is most famous for her diaries, which record over 40 years of her adventurous life.

Paddleford, Clementine (1900-1967) Born in Kansas, Clementine Paddleford was food editor of the *New York Herald-Tribune* from 1936 to 1966. From 1940 until her death, she contributed a weekly column on food to *This Week* magazine, a syndicated Sunday supplement available in newspapers throughout the United States. In order to reach far-flung culinary destinations, from lumberjacks' mess halls to state dinners, she learned to fly a plane. Paddleford was one of the most popular food editors in the world.

Paige, Satchel (1906-82). American baseball player. Born in Mobile, Alabama, Paige became legendary as a pitcher in the Negro Leagues. He joined the Cleveland Indians in 1948, after major league baseball was integrated. Although at 42 he was well past his prime, he helped Cleveland win the World Series. He was known for his wit as well as his impressive pitching.

Paine, Thomas (1737-1809). English-American writer and political theorist. Born in England, Paine had only the most rudimentary education. Though extremely poor, he set aside money for books and scientific equipment. After a series of failures and frustrations in England, he came to America with a letter of introduction from Benjamin Franklin, and found work editing the *Pennsylvania Magazine.* His pamphlet in support of American independence, *Common Sense,* sold more than 500,000 copies in a few months, and was important in paving the way for the Declaration of Independence. Paine volunteered in the war, but his greatest contribution was his 16 "Crisis" papers encouraging the patriot cause and boosting morale. Paine also raised money for the troops in America and in France. By the end of the Revolution, Paine was poverty-stricken. He had sold his popular writings cheaply, so as to reach a wide audience, and had made no profits. However, New York gave him a farm in New

Rochelle in recognition of his services, and Paine retired to pursue scientific inventions. In 1787, Paine went to Europe in connection with a bridge-building plan, but soon found himself drawn into political questions. In 1791, he published *Rights of Man*, defending the French Revolution. The book advocated republicanism, and progressive income taxation to fund old age pensions, relief for the poor, public education, and public works for the unemployed. The book was banned, and Paine indicted for treason. Paine fled to France, where he was imprisoned during the Reign of Terror. When he returned to the United States in 1892, he was ostracized for his criticism of religion in *The Age of Reason*, a deist work he had written in prison. He died in poverty, his contribution to the American Revolution nearly forgotten.

Pasteur, Louis (1822-95). French chemist and biologist. The son of a tanner, Pasteur grew up in the small town of Arbois, and studied physics and chemistry in Paris. His early research resulted in his discovery of molecular dissymmetry. His investigations into the fermentation of wine and beer while a professor at the University of Lille showed that fermentation was caused by microorganisms. Pasteur performed experiments that showed that microorganisms never arise from spontaneous generation. He also developed the germ theory of disease. With this new understanding of the origins of diseases, Pasteur contained epidemics, and developed vaccines against several diseases. He is the founder of the science of microbiology.

Peale, Norman Vincent (1898–1993). American clergyman. Born in Bowersville, Ohio, Peale became a Methodist minister in 1922. As pastor of New York City's Marble Collegiate Reformed Church from 1932 to 1984, Peale became famous for his sermons on a positive approach to modern life, which were broadcast over the radio. Peale's popular books include the 1952 self-help book *The Power of Positive Thinking*.

Peale, Ruth Stafford (1906-). American motivational speaker and author. Born in Fonda, Iowa, Ruth Stafford was the daughter of a minister. She married Dr. Norman Vincent Peale in 1930. She worked closely with her husband in many aspects of his ministry. She speaks and writes on religious and self-improvement themes. She is the founder and publisher of *Guideposts*, an interfaith magazine.

Picasso, Pablo (1881-1973). Spanish artist. Picasso studied art in Barcelona and Madrid, afterwards settling in France. A prolific artist of protean genius, Picasso worked in many different styles over the course of his career, his inventiveness shaping the course of 20th century art. His 1907 painting *Les Demoiselles d'Avignon,* with its flattened, fractured space and its stylized, distorted, and disturbing forms, was an important break with the conventions of painting, and a major step towards the development of cubism, a style Picasso helped invent. His post-cubist works include *Guernica,* a monumental, black-and-white work painted in protest of the fascist bombing of the Spanish town of the same name. Other works of Picasso draw on Greek myth, and often celebrate vital energy, sexuality, and pleasure.

Pindar (518-438 B.C.). Greek poet. Born to an aristocratic family, Pindar spent most of his life in Thebes. His extant works are 44 triumphal odes composed in honor of the victors of the four great national games. The odes were sung by choruses of young people at processions welcoming the victors home. Pindar was well traveled, and his poems express the spiritual and cultural unity of Greece that also found expression in the athletic games. The odes also tell stories from Greek mythology, and express deep religious and moral sentiments in complex language. Pindar is considered the greatest Greek lyric poet.

Plato (c.427-347 B.C.). Greek philosopher. Born to an aristocratic family in Athens, Plato became a disciple of Socrates. He later founded the Academy in Athens, where he taught mathematics and philosophy until his death. Plato's writings, which are in the form of dialogues, touch on nearly every problem that has concerned later philosophers. The early dialogues present the philosophy of Socrates. Dialogues of his middle and later period present Plato's own ideas. In the *Republic,* his major political work, Plato discusses the nature of justice, and sets forth his ideal state. In this and in the other great dialogues of Plato's middle years, Plato elaborates his theory of Forms, or Ideas. Forms are the unchanging archetypes that the objects in the physical world merely resemble. True knowledge must discover these perfect forms, not, as his famous cave metaphor would have it, their distorted shadows in the world of appearances. Plato has been one of the most influential thinkers in the history of Western civilization.

Plautus, Titus Maccius. (c.254–184 B.C.) Roman writer of comedies. Plautus' plays depicted middle class and lower class life with a flair for colloquial speech, situation and coarse humour. His plots and characters lived on in adaptations and imitations by playwrights such as Shakespeare and Moliére.

Pope, Alexander (1688–1744). English poet. Born in London as the son of a Roman Catholic linen merchant, Pope contracted a tubercular condition as a child, leaving him with shattered health, stunted growth, and a humpback. Catholics were barred from universities, and from the age of 12 Pope was self-educated. Pope wrote his first verses at 12, by 17 he was welcomed into London society as a prodigy, and his breakthrough work, *An Essay on Criticism* appeared when he was 23. Pope was a master of satire, and the greatest poet of the Enlightenment. His bitter literary quarrels are famous, but he also had many close friends.

Purkiser, W.T. (1910-92). American clergyman. A popular preacher in the Church of the Nazarene, W.T. Purkiser was a respected figure in the evangelical Christian community. His writings, which include *Beliefs that Matter Most,* are some of the most enduring works in the Holiness tradition.

Raddall, Thomas H. (1903-). English-Canadian novelist. Born in Kent, Raddall immigrated to Nova Scotia in 1913. He began writing while working in a paper mill. His first novel, *His Majesty's Yankees,* was set in Nova Scotia during the American Revolution. Raddall's novels are carefully researched portraits of Nova Scotia's history, customs, and life.

Rank, Otto (1884-1939). Austrian psychologist and psychotherapist. Born and educated in Vienna, Rank was one of the first students of Sigmund Freud. Rank's 1909 Freudian interpretation of myths, *Myth of the Birth of the Hero,* became a classic psychoanalytic work. He eventually broke away from Freud, and Rank's psychoanalytic theories exerted significant influence in the field.

Rayburn, Sam (1882-1961) U.S. Congressman. Raised on a Texas farm, Rayburn entered public life in 1907, when he was elected to the Texas legislature. He was elected to the U.S. House of Representatives in 1913, and served for more than 48 years. He was one of the main architects of the New Deal, and a dedicated Democrat. He was speaker of the House for 17 years.

Reade, Charles (1814–84). English novelist and dramatist. After attending Oxford, Reade became a barrister, and then turned to theater. His first success was *Masks and Faces,* an 1852 play about life in the theatre. Reade was passionate about social reform, and he penned a long series of novels propounding his views. The first was *It's Never Too Late to Mend,* about the harshness of prison life. His best novel, *The Cloister and the Hearth,* humorously relates the adventures of Gerard, the father of Erasmus.

Richter, Jean Paul(1763–1825). German novelist. Richter, a professor in Leipzig, Germany, won great popularity in his day for his warm, sentimental, and humorous writings. They include the romance *Hesperus and Siebenkäs* the tale of a man who ends his unhappy marriage by feigning death and burial.

Rilke, Rainer Maria (1875-1926). German writer. Born in Prague, in the present-day Czech Republic, Rilke had a lonely, troubled childhood. Later, he traveled extensively, basing himself in Paris until the outbreak of World War I. A trip to Russia, with its vast and inspiring landscape, and spiritually rich people, helped shape his religious outlook. Rilke's lifelong absorption in a search for spiritual and emotional fulfillment, and his preoccupation with death, find expression in his poetry.

Robson, Flora (McKenzie).(1902-84). English actress. Robson studied at the Royal Academy of Dramatic Art, London, and first appeared at the Shaftesbury Theatre, London, in 1921. She gained fame mainly in historical roles in plays and films, such as Queen Elizabeth in *Fire over England.* She consolidated her reputation with memorable stage performances in Shaw's *Captain Brassbound's Conversion* and Ibsen's *Ghosts.* She appeared in more than 60 films, and was created a dame in 1960.

Rockefeller, John D., III (1906-78). American philanthropist. The son of John D. Rockefeller, Jr., John D. Rockefeller III helped manage the family interests as well as participating in numerous philanthropies. A patron of the arts, he was one of the main sponsors and the first chairman of New York City's Lincoln Center for the Performing Arts.

Rockefeller, John D., Jr. (1874-1960). American industrialist. The son of the oil magnate and financier John D. Rockefeller, John D. Rockefeller Jr. took over the management of his father's business interests in 1911. He also planned and built Rockefeller center in New York City. His many philanthropies included the restoration of colonial Williamsburg,

Virginia, and the donation of the site for the United Nations international headquarters.

Roethke, Theodore (1908-63). American poet. Born in Saginaw, Michigan, Roethke wrote poetry that experimented with a wide variety of forms. He suffered two mental breakdowns in 1957, but overcame them to continue teaching and writing. He was at the height of his fame when he died from a coronary condition.

Rogers, Rutherford D. (1915-). American librarian. Born in Jesup, Iowa, Rogers is the university librarian at Yale University.

Rogers, Will (1879-1935). American entertainer. Born in Cherokee territory, in what eventually became Oklahoma, Rogers worked as a cowboy in his youth. He traveled in the U.S. and overseas performing in Wild West shows before settling in New York to work in vaudeville. He performed in the *Ziegfeld Follies* for several years, doing rope-tricks and delivering salty one-liners on politics and the talk of the day. He also performed on radio and in film, and wrote books, articles, and a syndicated column.

Rooney, Andy (1920-). American journalist and columnist. Rooney first won acclaim at age 24 as a correspondent in World War II. He writes a twice-weekly syndicated newspaper column, and is best known for his long-standing segment on the news program *60 Minutes*, where he puts forth his quirky take on life.

Rooney, Mickey (1922-). American actor. Born Joe Yule Jr. in Brooklyn, NY, Rooney, the son of actors, made his stage debut at the age of 15 months. He became a child star in the role of comic-strip character Mickey McGuire, which he played in some 50 silent films. He also starred as Andy Hardy in a series of 15 movies, and played opposite Judy Garland in several musicals. Other memorable films include 1935's *Boys Town*.

Roosevelt, Eleanor (1884–1962). American humanitarian. Born in New York City into a prominent family, Eleanor Roosevelt was orphaned at 10 and sent to boarding school in Britain. She married Franklin Delano Roosevelt in 1905, and while raising five children, was an active worker for women's organizations, social causes, and her husband's political campaigns. Influential in FDR's presidential administration, Eleanor Roosevelt worked for racial equality, women's rights, better housing, and employment. She was the United States delegate to the United Nations from 1945 to 1953, where she chaired the commission that drafted the Universal Declaration of Human Rights. Her dedication to helping humanity has won her love and respect around the world. She wrote a popular newspaper column "My Day," and many books, including *It's Up to the Women*, *The Moral Basis of Democracy* and *You Can Learn by Living*.

Roosevelt, Franklin Delano (1882–1945). United States president. Born in Hyde Park, New York into an old and wealthy family, Roosevelt, a lawyer, began his political career in 1910 when he was elected to the New York state senate. Roosevelt was part of the anti-Tammany, pro-reform wing of the Democratic Party. He served ably as Assistant Secretary of the Navy in Woodrow Wilson's administration, and made a vice presidential run in 1920. In 1921 he was stricken with poliomyelitis, leaving him paralyzed from the waist down. With unstinting effort he was able to regain partial use of his legs, but he remained crippled for life. With the support of his wife Eleanor, he reentered political life. In 1928 he was elected Governor of New York, and in 1932, at the height of the Great Depression, became president. The Roosevelt administration pushed large amounts of legislation through Congress to fight the Depression. Fashioned with the help of a "Brain Trust" of expert advisors, Roosevelt's New Deal was a vast, multi-faceted program. Finance and banking were reformed. Federal agencies were established to regulate industry. Public works programs were established to provide immediate employment, revive the economy by vast public spending, and develop rural areas of the country. Social security legislation was passed. Roosevelt was overwhelmingly elected to a second term. Although political opposition to his agenda had been initially defeated by Roosevelt's strong personality and the sheer pace of reforms, in the second term opposition strengthened, and reforms slowed. In Roosevelt's third term, the United States entered World War II. Roosevelt had been largely responsible for buildup of American military strength. Roosevelt died shortly before the end of the war. His presidency had forever changed the country.

Roosevelt, Theodore (1858-1919). American president. Born in New York City to a prominent, wealthy family, Roosevelt entered politics in 1882, when he served in the New York State legislature as a Republican. He rose in the party, and held federal offices. As Assistant Secretary to the Navy, Roosevelt, a fervent supporter of U.S.

expansion, worked to prepare the Navy for the Spanish-American War. When war came, he resigned his post to lead the volunteer regiment known as the Rough Riders. Returning from Cuba a popular hero, Roosevelt was elected Governor of New York. In 1900 he was elected Vice President, and a few months later, after the assassination of President McKinley, became President. Recognizing the popular demand for reform, Roosevelt initiated some 40 antitrust suits. His championship of the public interest, as well as his energetic and dramatic personality, captured the hearts of the American people, and he was elected to a second term. In his second term, he worked to regulate big business and to conserve public lands. An ardent expansionist, Roosevelt conducted an aggressive foreign policy, particularly in the pursuit of U.S. dominance of Latin America. He also played an active role in international affairs in general. His mediation of the Russo-Japanese war won him a Nobel Prize for Peace in 1906. Roosevelt was also a naturalist, explorer, and big game hunter.

Runes, Dagobert. (1902-82). American philosopher, editor, and author. Born in Bucovena, Rumania, Runes came to New York City in 1926, where he lectured and wrote on philosophy. In 1941 he founded the Philosophical Library, Inc., which published works by Albert Einstein, Bertrand Russell, and Jean-Paul Sartre, and others. Runes' writings include *Letters to My Son, The War Against Jews,* and *Philosophy for Everyman.*

Rusk, Dean (1909-94). U. S. secretary of state. Born in Georgia, Rusk served in the Far East during World War II, and joined the state department in 1945, becoming Assistant Secretary of State in 1949. He was Secretary of State under presidents Kennedy and Johnson. He later taught at the University of Georgia.

Russell, Bertrand (1872–1970). British philosopher, mathematician, and social reformer. Born in Wales into a prominent family, Russell was orphaned as a small child. He was brought up by a stern, puritanical grandmother, an experience that shaped his thinking on morality and education. A philosopher and mathematician, Russell was dismissed from his position as a lecturer at Cambridge, fined, and imprisoned because of his pacifism during World War I. Later, when the Nazis came to power, Russell abandoned his pacifist position, but after the war again became a leading spokesman for pacifism, particularly nuclear disarmament. Russell strove to base his thought - mathematical, philosophical, and ethical - on actual experience. This is evident not only in his philosophy but in his pacifism, which was responsive to the justice of particular wars. Undogmatic, an ethical relativist, and a firm believer in the ultimate power of rationality, Russell objected to religion because belief based on faith instead of evidence was incompatible with his vision of knowledge. He believed that cruelty and violence had their roots in childhood experience, and that pacifism, just relations between the sexes, and other social goals could not be achieved without major changes in education. In 1927 he and his wife, Dora, founded the experimental Beacon Hill School, which influenced schools in Britain and America. His work in philosophy influenced the course of the discipline in Britain. He remained active in social causes all his life.

Russell, Bill (1934-). American basketball player, coach, and sports announcer. Born in Monroe, Louisiana, Russell played on the University of San Francisco basketball team and the United States Olympic team before joining the Boston Celtics, and launching them on a string of NBA championships. In 1966, Russell became a player-coach for the Celtics, the first black head coach in major league professional sports, and won two more championships before he retired in 1969. Russell later coached the Seattle SuperSonics and the Sacramento Kings.

Sa'di (c. 1213 – c. 1292). Persian poet. Born Musilh al-Din in Shiraz, Iran, Sa'di studied in Baghdad and traveled widely. He is renowned for his lyric poetry in Arabic and Persian. His most famous works were *The Orchard,* a verse collection of fables illustrating Islamic virtues, and the collection of stories and maxims *The Rose Garden.*

Saint-Exupéry, Antoine de (1900–1944). French aviator and writer. In 1926, Saint-Exupéry became a commercial pilot and published his first story. Works such as *Wind Sand and Stars* and *Night Flight* are based on his experiences flying over Europe, Africa, and South America. His poetic, evocative writing express his sensitivity to nature and his love of freedom and of the life of the mind. During World War II he was a military pilot and was lost in action. His last book, *The Little Prince,* is a fable beloved by adults and children.

Sandburg, Carl (1878–1967). American poet and biographer. Born in Galesburg, Illinois to poor Swedish immigrants, Sandburg left school to work at the age of 13. After serving in the Spanish American War, he attended college in his hometown and then went to work for a

Milwaukee newspaper. From 1910 to 1912 he was secretary to the Socialist mayor of Milwaukee. Sandburg later moved to Chicago, where he became an editorial writer for the Chicago Daily News. With the appearance of volumes of verse such as 1916's *Chicago*, his reputation was established. Sandburg drew inspiration from American history and was influenced by Walt Whitman. Like Whitman, Sandburg often celebrates ordinary people and things. Sandburg's most ambitious work was his six-volume biography of Abraham Lincoln; it exalts Lincoln as the symbol and embodiment of the American spirit. The last four volumes won the Pulitzer Prize.

Santayana, George (1863-1952). American philosopher and poet. Born in Madrid, Santayana moved to Boston in 1872. He taught philosophy at Harvard from 1889 to 1912, when he returned to Europe. In works such as *The Life of Reason* Santayana investigates the relationship between the mind and reality.

Sarton, May (1912-95). American writer. Born in Belgium, Sarton immigrated to the United States at age four. At 17 she joined a theatre company as an actress. She began publishing her poetry when still very young, and to lecture and teach at universities in order to support her writing. She was the author of many novels and books of poetry. Her series of journals describing her solitary writer's life in a house on the Maine coast, beginning with 1973 *Journal of Solitude,* brought her wide readership, particularly women who identified with her efforts to carve out an independent life.

Sartre, Jean-Paul (1905-1980). French philosopher and writer. Born in Paris, and educated in Switzerland and Berlin, Sartre worked as a teacher, served as a soldier in World War II, and was active in the French Resistance. During the occupation, he wrote his first plays, *The Flies* and *No Exit,* and his major work of philosophy, *Being and Nothingness.* Sartre's thought is influenced by German philosophy, especially Heidegger. Sartre was a leading exponent of existentialism. He emphasized man's complete freedom, and consequent total personal responsibility. After World War II, Sartre founded the political and literary magazine *Les Temps Modernes.*

Schiller, Friedrich von (1759-1805). Schiller was the son of an army captain in the service of the Duke of Wurtumburg. The Duke forced Schiller, who hated military life, to become an army surgeon, and became furious when Schiller wrote *The Robbers,* a play attacking political tyranny. Forbidden by the Duke to write, Schiller fled the Duchy and became a dramatist at the Mannheim theatre. In later years, Schiller wrote philosophy, history, and poetry as well as plays. He had to struggle against poor health throughout his life, and always maintained the spirit of liberty so evident in his work. His dramas exemplify his idealism and love of freedom. He is considered the greatest German dramatist.

Schlesinger, Arthur Meier Jr. (1917–). American historian and public official. Born in Columbus, Ohio, Schlesinger's parents were involved in progressive social causes. During World War II Schlesinger served with the Office of War Information and the Office of Strategic Services. He was Professor of History at Harvard from 1946 to 1961. He won the 1945 Pulitzer prize in history for *The Age of Jackson*; in 1965 he won the Pulitzer prize in biography for *A Thousand Days*, his portrait of the Kennedy administration. Schlesinger served as a special assistant to the president in the Kennedy White House. In 1967, Schlesinger was appointed Albert Schweitzer Chair in the Humanities at the City University of New York Graduate School.

Schuller, Robert H. (1926-). American Protestant minister and television evangelist. The son of an Iowa farmer, Schuller was ordained in 1950 and in 1955 converted a drive-in movie theatre into a church. Since 1970, Schuller's televised "Hour of Power" has become one of the top religious broadcasts in America. He is also the author of motivational books.

Schulz, Charles M. (1922-2000). American cartoonist. Born in St. Paul, Minnesota, Schulz studied art after seeing a 'Do you like to Draw ?' ad. His syndicated comic strip *Peanuts* ran for fifty years, until the day of his death. The gentle humor of *Peanuts* is loved around the world.

Schumacher, E.F. (1911-77). German economist. Interned in Britain while at Oxford University at the outbreak of World War II, Schumacher served as the economic adviser to the British Control Commission in Germany after the war. In his book *Small is Beautiful* Schumacher expressed his concern for Third World peoples caught up in the maelstrom of industrial development. He founded the Intermediate Technology Group to promote culturally appropriate and humane technologies.

Seneca (c. 4 B.C.-A.D. 65) Roman philosopher, dramatist, and statesman. Born in Corduba (now Córdoba, Spain), Seneca went to Rome to study. He became famous as an orator while still a youth. Later, as tutor of the young Emperor Nero, he was the virtual ruler of the Roman world. He wrote moral essays, reflecting his Stoic philosophy, and also nine plays, which had a strong influence on Renaissance drama.

Shakespeare, William (1564-1616). Born in Stratford-on-Avon, Shakespeare moved to London around 1588, and by 1592 had established himself as a playwright and actor. His plays and poems were popular, and he was able to earn a comfortable living. Since his death, his plays have been almost continuously performed. Shakespeare's plays, with their complex characters, and their poetry, eloquence, and unparalleled use of language, are some of literature's greatest achievements.

Shaw, George Bernard (1856-1950). Irish writer. Born in Dublin, Shaw had to quit school at 14 to work at a clerical job. In 1876 he moved to London, where he lived precariously from odd jobs and occasional publication of his novels and journalism. A fervent socialist, he became popular as a public speaker. He wrote arts criticism, and began writing plays, which were beginning to be produced when he married Charlotte Payne-Townsend, an Irish heiress, in 1898. Shaw's vigorous dramas of ideas reshaped the British stage, which at the time was still dominated by Victorian melodramas. In plays such as *Pygmalion* and *Major Barbara* Shaw combined social criticism and moral and intellectual complexity with brilliantly witty dialogue and the verve of an old-fashioned comedy of manners. One of the greatest British playwrights, he won the Nobel Prize for literature in 1925.

Sheehy, Gail. (1937-). American author. Born in Mamaroneck, New York, Sheehy has been a magazine writer and editor. She is best known for her books that address stages of life, such as *Passages*.

Sheperd, Odell (1884-1967). American writer, professor, and politician. Born in Illinois, Shepard was a professor of English for 30 years. He served as Lieutenant Governor of Connecticut from 1940 to 1941. The author of novels and nonfiction, he received the Pulitzer Prize in 1937 for his biography of A. Bronson Alcott, *Pedlar's Progress*.

Siegel, Bernie, M.D. (1932-). A former surgeon at Yale New Haven Hospital, Siegal is the author of books such as *Love, Medicine and*

Miracles. He examines the link between spirituality and health and stresses the idea that we must take responsibility for our health. Siegal's aims include humanizing medical care and medical education.

Simonides (c. 556-c. 468 B.C.). Greek poet. As a young man, Simonides studied music on the island of Ceos, but he lived most of his life in Athens. He became famous for his poetry lauding the heroes and battles of the Greek wars against the Persians. Simonides wrote in a great variety of poetic forms - epigrams, elegies, odes, choral lyric works – but little of his work survives today.

Simpson, Alan (1931-). American politician. Simpson represented Wyoming in the U.S. Senate from 1978 to 1996. He was party whip from 1984 on. Simpson, known for his conservative politics and his blunt humor, published a political memoir and critique of the news media, *Right in the Old Gazoo: A Lifetime of Scrapping with the Press,* in 1997.

Singer, Isaac Bashevis (1904–91). American writer. Born in Poland, Singer immigrated to the United States in 1935 and became a journalist for the *Jewish Daily Forward* in New York. His novels and short stories, all written in Yiddish, draw on Jewish folklore, often containing elements of fantasy. He became an American citizen in 1943, and in 1978 was the fist Yiddish-language author to win the Nobel Prize in Literature. His works include *Satan in Goray,* a novel dealing with religious intolerance in Poland; *Gimpel the Fool,* a collection of short stories; books for children and several plays.

Smith, Adam (1723–90). Scottish economist and philosopher. Educated at Glasgow and Oxford, Smith was a professor of moral philosophy at the University of Glasgow. In 1776 he published his seminal *Wealth of Nations.* Smith believed that a free market is the optimal condition for the production and distribution of wealth; in a laissez-faire, or free trade, economy, the pursuit of self-interest brings about the public welfare. Smith has been extremely influential on later economists.

Socrates (c. 469-399 B.C.) Greek philosopher. Socrates was known for his wisdom before he was 40, when the oracle at Delphi proclaimed that he was the wisest man in Greece. Socrates felt that he was charged with a mission to seek wisdom, for the moral and intellectual improvement of himself and his countrymen. He believed that knowledge and virtue were identical. Since evil results from ignorance, philosophy should be the task of every person. Socrates spent his time in the streets and the marketplaces, engaging ordinary citizens in discussions on virtue, justice, and piety. Although he had been a military hero, he never sought public office, for fear of being forced to compromise his principles. He criticized injustices committed by the government without regard to his personal safety. When he was put on trial for impiety, he refused to disavow his principals or to seek safety in exile. He is famous as a person who stayed true to his principles at the cost of his life.

Solon (c.639-c.559 B.C.). Athenian statesman. Solon was elected to Athens' highest office in 594, a time when the unchecked power of the nobility was driving the peasants into debt, landlessness, and serfdom. Solon instituted land reform, and put an end to serfdom. He replaced the law code of Draco with more humane laws, and made important constitutional changes, such as opening the Athenian assembly to all freemen. Solon's reforms became the basis of the Athenian state. He was also a poet.

Solzhenitsyn, Aleksandr (1918–). Russian writer. A Red Army artillery captain decorated for bravery during World War II, Solzhenitsyn was serving at the German front in 1945 when he was arrested for criticizing Stalin in letters to a friend. He spent eight years in forced labor camps, and three more years in exile, until his citizenship was restored in 1956. His first novels describe the grimness of life in the vast labor-camp system. Solzhenitsyn's subsequent works, also critical of Soviet society, were banned in the Soviet Union, but were circulated underground, and read widely abroad as well. Over time, pressure on Solzhenitsyn increased. The government compelled him to decline the 1970 Nobel Prize. Following the foreign publication of *The Gulag Archipelago*, a detailed non-fiction account of the network of Soviet prison and labor camps, Solzhenitsyn was arrested, accused of treason, and expelled from the Soviet Union. He lived in Switzerland and then in Vermont, where he wrote a series of works dealing with the history of the Russian revolution. After the fall of the Soviet Union, Solzhenitsyn returned to Russia as a very popular and visible public figure.

Stark, Freya (1893-1993). Explorer and travel writer. Born in Paris and educated in London, Dame Freya Stark boldly traveled through the forbidden territory of the Syrian Druze in 1928. She recorded her adventures in *The Valley of the Assassins*. She went on to a lifetime of exploration, mainly in the Middle East, and wrote over 20 books. During the 30s, Stark discovered the incense trade routes of the ancient world in the little-explored outback of Saudi Arabia. When she was in her 60s she explored the trails upon which Alexander the Great had marched, resulting in three of her best known books, *The Lycian Shore, Ionia: A Quest* and *Alexander's Path*. Stark lived to be 100.

Stevenson, Adlai (1900–1965). American statesman. The grandson of a Vice President, Stevenson's government career began with federal agency posts in the New Deal era. Even in the early 1930s, he was most interested in international affairs. He fought American isolationism at the start of World War II, and later participated in the founding of the United Nations. He served as a U. N. delegate in 1946 and 1947. In 1949, Stevenson was elected Democratic Governor of Illinois by an unprecedented majority. His reforms in office brought him national attention. He unsuccessfully ran for president against Dwight D. Eisenhower in 1952, and again in 1956. In 1960 he lost the Democratic presidential nomination to John F. Kennedy. From 1961 until his death, Stevenson served as U.S. Ambassador to the United Nations. Despite his defeats at the ballot box, Stevenson was admired and respected as an eloquent speaker and a champion of liberal reform and internationalism.

Stevenson, Robert Louis (1850-94). Scottish writer. Born and educated in Edinburgh, Stevenson travelled extensively in warmer climes, seeking relief from his tuberculosis. His first writings recount his travels. He also wrote poems and essays, but he is famous for his adventure and fantasy novels, which include *Treasure Island* and *Doctor Jekell and Mr. Hyde*. Stevenson contributed another classic to children"s literature in *A Child's Garden of Verses*, which contains some of his best-known poems. Stevenson lived briefly in America, where he married. He and his wife settled in Samoa in a last attempt to save his health. He died there five years later.

Stoppard, Tom (1937-). English playwright. Born Tomas Straussler in Czechoslovakia, in 1946 he settled in Bristol with his mother and his British stepfather, whose surname he adopted. Stoppard quit school to work as a journalist in 1954. In 1960, he moved to London, where he became a theatre critic and began writing plays. Stoppard's plays, which include *Rosencrantz and Guildenstern are Dead, Jumpers* and *Arcadia,* are witty and structurally complex.

Stout, Rex (1886–1975). American writer. Born in Noblesville, Indiana, Stout served in the navy and founded Vanguard Press in New York City. He is best known for his detective stories,

Strunsky, Simeon (1879-1948). American writer. Born in Russia, Strunsky graduated from Columbia University in 1900 worked on the staff of the *New International Encyclopedia* and the New York *Evening Post*. In the 30s and 40s he wrote the column "Topics of the Times" in the *New York Times*. His journalism and essays describe American culture and life in New York City.

Tallentyre, S.G. (1868-1919). English author. Tallentyre wrote a life of Voltaire and *The Money-Spinner and Other Character Notes*.

Temple, Shirley (1928-). American actress. Born in Santa Monica, California, Temple appeared in her first film at age three. The curly-haired, tap-dancing little girl became famous in 1934, when she starred in four films. During the second half of the thirties, Temple was the biggest box-office draw in Hollywood. She retired from acting in 1949. In 1967 she made an unsuccessful run for Congress, and in 1969 was a member of the United States delegation to the United Nations. Later, she served as ambassador to Ghana and to Czechoslovakia.

Tennyson , Alfred, Lord (1809-1892). English poet. Son of a Lincolnshire clergyman, Tennyson began writing poetry in his early teens. In 1831 his father died, and Tennyson became responsible for his family and its precarious finances. Two years later he was overwhelmed by the death of a close friend. Tennyson's next published book of poems expressed his doubts in a materialistic, increasingly scientific age and his longing for religious faith. In 1850 he published *In Memoriam,* an elegy sequence recording Tennyson's years of doubt and spiritual searching in the wake of his friend's death. That same year he was appointed poet laureate, and, after a courtship that had been extended over a decade due to his precarious finances, was finally able to marry. His later poetry includes *Idylls of the King,* a group of poems about King Arthur. In 1883 Tennyson was created a peer and occupied a seat in the House of Lords. For most of his career, he was acclaimed by the critics and loved by the general public.

Teresa, Mother (1910-97). Catholic missionary. Born Agnes Goxha Bojaxhiu in Skopje, in present-day Macedonia, Mother Teresa felt since childhood that she had a vocation to help the poor. At 17, she became a nun and began teaching at a Calcutta convent school. In 1948, she left the school to teach homeless children. After four years of working with the poor in the slums of Calcutta, Mother Teresa, who had attracted church and municipal funding and the help of volunteers, founded the Missionaries of Charity. This order operates orphanages, schools, homes for the dying, nutrition programs, disaster relief, and other support for the poor. It comprises about 1,000 brothers and sisters in India, and is now active in more than 90 countries. Mother Teresa won the 1979 Nobel Peace Prize.

Thomas Aquinas, Saint (1225-74). Italian philosopher and theologian. Thomas's family ruled a small feudal domain. They were so opposed to their son's decision to become a Dominican friar that they abducted him and held him captive for a year. Thomas held out, and after his release studied and eventually taught in the great university center of the Dominicans in Paris. At this time, there was a great influx of classical and Arabic science and philosophy coming into Paris. St. Thomas Aquinas's great achievement was to integrate the recently discovered philosophy of Aristotle into Christianity. Participating in an important doctrinal struggle of the day over the relationship between reason and faith, he developed a systematic philosophy that held reason to operate autonomously, yet in the light of faith. Controversial in its time, his philosophy is now officially recognized by the Catholic Church.

Thoreau, Henry David (1817-1862). American author and naturalist. Born in Concord, Massachusetts, Thoreau attended Harvard University. There he first read the works of Ralph Waldo Emerson, who later became his mentor. In 1845 Thoreau built a hut by Walden Pond. He lived there for the next two years in near-solitude, occupying himself with the observation of nature, contemplation, and the basic labor needed for survival. His famous book *Walden* records this experience and expresses his philosophy. A transcendentalist, Thoreau emphasized independence, closeness with nature, and freedom from materialism. Thoreau was later imprisoned for his refusal to pay poll tax, in protest against the Mexican war. Out of that experience he wrote "Civil Disobedience," an essay that influenced Gandhi and Martin Luther King Jr.

Thurber, James (1894–1961) American writer and cartoonist. Born in Columbus, Ohio, Thurber, after working at various newspapers, became a staff writer at the *New Yorker* magazine in 1927. His cartoons and whimsical, ironic stories helped shape the tone of that magazine. Collections of his drawings and writings include *My Life and Hard Times* and *Thurber's Dogs*.

Tillich, Paul (1886-1965). German-American theologian. Born and educated in Germany, Tillich immigrated to the United States after his opposition to the Nazis cost him his position as a theology professor at various German universities. He taught theology at Union Theological Seminary and other American universities. Tillich's theology incorporated depth psychology and existentialist philosophy. His writings include *The Courage To Be*.

Tolkein, J.R.R. (1892–1973). Engliish writer. A respected medieval scholar, Tolkien is famous for his series of fantasy novels, *The Hobbit* and *The Lord of the Rings*. The books take place in the imaginary world of Middle Earth. The astounding breadth and detail of Tolkien's creation included the invention of several languages, a history, and a cosmology. The books shaped the fantasy genre and inspired a vast and devoted readership.

Tolstoy, Leo (1828-1910). Russian writer. Born on his noble family's country estate, Tolstoy was orphaned at nine and raised by his aunts. At age 16 he went to university. Bored by his classes, he left without receiving a degree. In his twenties, he divided his time between an extravagant life in Moscow and St. Petersburg and managing his estate, where he began several unsuccessful projects to aid and educate his serfs. He also served in the army, and began writing novels, beginning with the autobiographical *Childhood* in 1852. In 1862 Tolstoy married, and began a large family. During this time he wrote his masterpieces, *War and Peace,* an epic novel set in the Napoleonic wars, and *Anna Karenina,* the story of a woman's doomed attempts to defy society and in an adulterous love affair. Around 1876, Tolstoy's lifelong philosophical questioning and self-examination came to a head, and he underwent a spiritual conversion. He devoted the rest of his life to practicing and preaching his new philosophy, based on what he considered the essence of Christianity: universal love and nonresistance in the face of evil. In works such as *What I Believe In*, Tolstoy urged people to follow their own consciences, rather than the dictates of religion or state, he condemned all forms of violence, and he advocated simplicity of life and living from one's own labor. Tolstoy's ideas gained followers around the world. His novels are considered among the greatest ever written.

Tomlin, Lily (1939-). American actress and comedienne. Born in Detroit, Tomlin began appearing on the television variety show *Rowan and Martin's Laugh-In* in 1969. Her long film career includes the 1980 hit *Nine to Five*. She has also co-written and performed *In Search for Signs of Intelligent Life in the Universe*, a one-woman Broadway show.

Toynbee, Arnold (1852–83). English economic historian, philosopher, and reformer. A tutor at Oxford, Toynbee was active in reform work, particularly among the London poor. A pioneer in the social settlement movement, the first settlement house in the world was named for him. Toynbee's lectures to workingmen were published as *Lectures on the Industrial Revolution of the 18th Century in England*, a pioneer work in economic history.

Truman, Harry S. (1884-1972). Born in Missouri, Truman grew up on a farm. He worked at odd jobs, eventually becoming a successful farmer. After serving in World War I, Truman married a girl he had known since childhood and opened a clothing store. When the business failed he entered Missouri politics. Although he had the support of the local Democratic machine, Truman fought corruption while in office. He also attended law school. In 1934 he was elected to the United States Senate, where he firmly supported the New Deal. In his second term he gained national attention as chairman of a Senate committee investigating fraud and waste in defense contracts. In 1944 he was elected Vice President, and a few months later, upon the death of President Roosevelt, became President. He negotiated the postwar settlement in Europe and authorized the dropping of the atomic bomb to end the conflict with Japan. Under Truman's administration America initiated a policy of containment towards the Soviet Union, implemented the Marshall Plan for the reconstruction of Europe, joined the North Atlantic Treaty Organization and the United Nations, and entered the Korean War. In domestic affairs Truman promoted the continuation of New Deal-type social welfare programs, but much of his legislation was defeated. He also worked to end racial discrimination, desegregating the armed forces in 1948.

Twain, Mark (1835-1910). Born Samuel Clemens, Twain was apprenticed at 12 to a printer in the Mississippi town of Hannibal, Missouri. He began writing for his brother's newspaper there. After several years as a pilot on the Mississippi river and several failed get-rich-quick schemes, he became a newspaperman in San Francisco. He began publishing humorous short stories and sketches, and was soon in demand for lecture tours. After his marriage in 1879, he settled in Hartford, Connecticut. There he produced his best work, including *Huckleberry Finn*. In this story of an independent young boy and a runaway slave floating down the Mississippi on a raft, Twain created a realistic portrait of 19th century America, bringing to bear his gifts for characterization and keen social observation as well as humor. After the deaths of his daughters and wife, his writing ceased to be humorous and became somber.

van Buren, Abigail (1918 –). Advice columnist. Born Pauline Esther Friedman, Van Buren began her career in 1956, when she told the editor of the San Francisco *Chronicle* she could write a better advice column than the one they ran. "Dear Abby" was an instant success. Today it is among the most widely syndicated newspaper columns in the world.

van Gogh, Vincent (1853-90). Dutch painter. The son of a pastor, van Gogh grew up in a rural village in southern Holland. At 16 he was apprenticed to a Hague art dealer, where he developed an eye for painting. Later, impelled by a desire to help humanity, he worked as a missionary among oppressed coal-miners. He came in conflict with the church authorities, and underwent a spiritual crisis. It was then that he began to draw seriously, deciding in 1880 that his way of helping humanity was through art. His early paintings, such as 1885's *The Potato Eaters,* were somber-hued studies of peasant life, reflecting van Gogh's concern for the oppressed and the poor. In 1886 he went to Paris to live with his brother Theo, an art dealer. There he met Pissarro, Seurat, Gauguin, and other postimpressionist painters. Their influence led van Gogh to abandon his somber palette and traditional style. He developed a personal idiom of expressive brushwork, vigorous contours, and striking colors. After two years in Paris, he went to Arles. There, surrounded by nature and the bright colors of southern France, he painted some of his greatest works. After a year, however, he began to suffer bouts of madness. He spent the next few years in an asylum and under the care of his brother in Paris, painting all the while. Finally, despairing of a cure, he shot himself. Although unknown during his lifetime, he was later recognized as a great painter.

Van Horne, William (1843-1915). American-born Canadian railway official. Van Horne worked for U.S. railroad companies before directing the construction of Canada's first trans-continental railroad

van Zeller, Hubert (1905-1984) Dom Hubert van Zeller was a popular spiritual director and a prolific author. In books such as *Spirit of Penance, Path to God* van Zeller gave practical advice on how to incorporate spirituality into daily life.

Virgil (70 B.C.) Roman poet. Born in the countryside near Mantua, Italy, Virgil was the son of a farmer. He studied in Milan, Naples, and Rome, and then returned to his father's farm. 10 years later, after his family lost their land in the civil war, Virgil settled in Rome. He devoted his life to writing poetry. His *Ecologues* and his *Georgics* celebrate rural life. Some of these poems are arcadian idealizations of the countryside. Others adapt the pastoral mode to describe real life and work on the farm, or, reflecting Virgil's own experience, to express the sorrow of dispossessed farmers. After the destructive civil wars came to an end in 31 B.C., Virgil began the epic poem for which he is best known. The *Aeneid* celebrates the glory and destiny of Rome, and embodies the values of the peaceful and triumphant Augustan age. Virgil died after working on the *Aeneid* for 11 years, leaving it incomplete. Contemporaries admired Virgil's poetry for its expression of the noblest of Roman ideals, as well as for its poetic perfection. Virgil's fame has endured, and he has had significant influence on European literature.

Voltaire (1694-1778). French writer. Born François-Marie Arouet, he wrote tragedies and epic poems under the pen name Voltaire. He won great acclaim as a writer, and also as the wit of Paris society, coining widely quoted epigrams. His witticisms, when directed at powerful men, twice landed him in prison. He was released the second time upon a promise to go to England. There he met many men of letters. He admired the liberty enjoyed in England, and was influenced by John Locke. Much of Voltaire's vast oeuvre, which included poems, dramas, romances, histories, and philosophical works, has been forgotten, but some of his writings, such as his *Dictionnaire Philosophique,* a compendium of his thought on a wide variety of subjects, and his satirical novel *Candide,* are still widely read today. In all his varied works, Voltaire, a central figure of the Enlightenment, champions reason, science, religious tolerance, the rights of man, and impartial justice.

Walker, Alice. (1944-). Born to a family of poor sharecroppers in

Georgia, Walker attended Spellman College and Sarah Lawrence College. She eventually moved to Mississippi, where she and her husband, a civil rights lawyer, faced physical threats because of their interracial marriage. Walker published poems and novels, and taught literature at several colleges, including one of the first women's literature courses in the nation. In the course of her research, she rediscovered the work of a forgotten Harlem Rennaissance author, Zora Neale Hurston. Walker's writing draws on her experience of black life in the South, her participation in the civil rights movement, and her travels in Africa. Her 1982 novel *The Color Purple* won the Pulitzer Prize.

Wallace, Mike (1918-). American journalist. Born in Brookline, Massachusetts, Wallace began his radio and television career as an announcer and an actor. After serving as a naval communications officer in World War II, he continued acting and also worked as a talk show host and a radio news reporter. In 1955 he began anchoring television news. The next year, Wallace came to prominence as a hard-hitting interviewer and investigative reporter of *Night Beat*. He became a news correspondent for various television networks, covering Vietnam and the Nixon campaign. In 1968 he became co-editor and co-host of the CBS news magazine *60 Minutes*. In this mainstay of television news, Wallace continues to bring audiences probing interviews with top newsmakers, and revealing investigative reports.

Warren, Earl (1891-1974). Chief Justice of the United States. Born in Los Angeles, Warren was Governor of California before President Dwight D. Eisenhower appointed him Chief Justice of the U.S. Supreme Court in 1953. Under Warren's leadership, the court made landmark decisions in the areas of civil rights and individual liberties. These decisions included Brown v. the Board of Education in 1954, which desegregated the schools and decisions in criminal cases protecting the rights of the accused. Warren also headed the commission that investigated the assassination of President Kennedy. He retired in 1969.

Washington, George (1732-99). United States president. Born to a wealthy Virginia family, Washington served in the French and Indian wars, rising to Commander in Chief of the Virginia militia. Afterwards, he became a leader in the Virginian opposition to British colonial policy. During the American Revolution he was Commander in Chief of the Continental army. Over the course of a campaign beset with challenges, Washington transformed untrained, ill-equipped troops into an effective army who bore him great personal loyalty. After the war was won, Washington presided over the Constitutional Convention, and was unanimously chosen to be the nation's first president. In his two terms as president, he strove to avoid partisan struggle.

Wayne, John. (1907–79). American movie actor. Born Marian Michael Morrison in Winterset, Iowa, Wayne had been appearing in westerns for about ten years when his leading role in John Ford's *Stagecoach* earned him great fame. Playing the roles of cowboys and soldiers – tough, rugged and taciturn, but honest and idealistic - Wayne came to represent a certain American masculine ideal. He won an Academy Award in 1969 for *True Grit*.

White, E.B. (1899-1985). American writer. Born Elwyn Brooks White in Mount Vernon, New York, White was on the staff of the *New Yorker* magazine in its early days, where he wrote columns for "The Talk of the Town" section. A keen observer of his world, and a witty and graceful writer, White is the author of books such as *Here is New York* as well as children's classics such as *Charlotte's Web*.

Whitehead, Alfred North (1861–1947). English mathematician and philosopher. A lecturer in mathematics at Cambridge and the University of London, and later a professor of philosophy at Harvard, Whitehead has made contributions to mathematics and logic, the philosophy of science, and the study of metaphysics. Whitehead criticized traditional categories of philosophy for failing to convey the essential interrelation of matter, space, and time. Whitehead's thought as applied to religion offered a concept of God as interdependent with the world and developing with it, rather than a perfect and omnipotent God. His works include *Process and Reality* and *Science and the Modern World*.

Whitman, Walt (1819-92). American poet. Whitman grew up in Brooklyn, New York. He left school at 12 to learn the printing trade, later becoming a journalist. He was editor of a prominent Brooklyn newspaper for two years, until his vehement advocacy of abolition and the "free-soil" movement cost him his job. In 1855 Whitman published *Leaves of Grass* at his own expense. The 12 poems of *Leaves of Grass*, written in free verse and filled with incantatory rhythms, sing the praises of the body, the self, democracy, and common things. They were completely unlike the poetry of the time. *Leaves of Grass*, initially rejected, eventually became the most influential volume of poems in the history of American literature.

Whittier, John Greenleaf (1807-92). American poet. Born near Haverhill, Massachusetts, Whittier received little education, but read widely. He began writing poetry at 14. For over a decade, Whittier contributed poems and articles to newspapers and magazines. Whittier was a Quaker and a fervent abolitionist. He served in the Massachusetts legislature, ran for Congress, and was a founder of the Republican party. He published many volumes of his poems, which portray New England life in loving detail.

Wilde, Oscar (1854-1900). Irish-born writer. Wilde grew up in the atmosphere of wit, brilliance, and literary talk of his mother's Dublin salon. As a student at Oxford, he excelled in classics, wrote poetry, and was known for his eccentricity and wit. Although he and his circle of aesthetes were satirized in the press, his poems, stories, novels, and essays were well received. His best works were his brilliantly witty, epigram-filled plays, such as *The Importance of Being Earnest.*

Williams, Ted (1918-). American baseball player. Born in San Diego, Williams was a left-handed outfielder with the Boston Red Sox from 1939 to 1960. He won the Triple Crown twice, and had a .344 lifetime batting average, with .406 in 1941. He interrupted his career to serve five years as a flyer in World War II. He managed the Washington Senators from 1969 to 1972.

Williams, Tennessee (1911-83). American playwright. Born Thomas Lanier Williams in Columbus, Missouri, Williams began writing plays while a university student. He wrote plays and worked at jobs ranging from St. Louis shoe factory worker to theatre usher to Hollywood scriptwriter. In 1944, the success of *The Glass Menagerie* enabled him to write full time. Most of Williams' plays examine decayed Southern gentility and the frustration, lies, violence, and sex that lie beneath a thin social veneer.

Wilson, Woodrow (1856–1924). United States president. Born in Staunton, Virginia, Wilson became a professor of jurisprudence and political economy at Princeton and eventually university president. In 1910, he became governor of New Jersey. Despite much resistance from the establishment, he pushed important reforms through the state legislature. He was elected president in 1912. He began a series of

"New Freedom" reforms, which included regulating labor conditions, curbing monopolies, and women's suffrage. At the outbreak of World War I, Wilson strove to maintain American neutrality. Faced with German attacks on American shipping, Wilson ultimately decided to go to war. An eloquent speaker, his addresses did much to rally the country behind the war effort. Wilson was an idealist, and believed that the United States could bring liberty and peace to the world. He set out for postwar peace conferences in Europe hoping to create a settlement that would create a world of lasting peace, governed by the self-determination of peoples and international justice. The Treaty of Versailles fell far short of his dream, but establish one key priority, the League of Nations. When Wilson returned home, bitter quarrels broke out in the Republican-controlled Congress over the League, which opponents felt weakened U.S. sovereignty. Congress never ratifed the treaty, and Wilson, fatigued and stressed, suffered a stroke from which he never recovered.

Winfrey, Oprah (1954-). American talk-show host. Born in Kosciusko, Mississippi, Winfrey overcame a childhood of neglect and abuse to become an excellent student and a television newscaster, and ultimately a talk show host. *The Oprah Winfrey Show* was nationally syndicated in 1986. The same year Oprah formed Harpo productions to produce the show and her other projects. In 2000, she launched *O: The Oprah Magazine.* Winfrey has also acted in several films, including *The Color Purple,* for which she received an Academy Award nomination. Winfrey's many devoted fans respond to her openness both in dealing with controversial issues on her talk show and in telling her own story, with its challenges and dark moments and its impressive achievements.

Wolfe, Thomas (1900-38). American novelist. The son of a stonecutter and a boardinghouse keeper, Wolfe was born and raised in Asheville, North Carolina. The town, his parents, and his childhood experience of the rural south later became the basis of his novels. After studying at the University of North Carolina, Woolfe moved to New York City intending to become a playwright. Instead, he taught at New York University, wrote *Look Homeward, Angel,* a novel which has become an American classic, and worked on several more novels, which were published, incomplete, after his early death.

Wong, Jan (1953-). Canadian journalist. Jan Wong is an award-winning reporter for the Toronto *Globe and Mail. Red China Blues: My*

Long March from Mao to Now is the memoir of her experiences in China, beginning with her sojourn there as an idealistic 19 year old Maoist exchange student, through her disillusionment with the Cultural Revolution and growing sympathy for Chinese dissenters, up until her coverage of Tiananmen square massacres as the *Globe's* Beijing correspondent.

Wordsworth, William (1770–1850). English poet. Born in Cumberland, Wordsworth traveled abroad after graduating from Cambridge. In France, he was strongly influenced by the ideals of the Revolution. Upon returning to England, Wordsworth settled in Dorcetshire with his sister, who was his devoted companion and helper throughout his life. In Dorcetshire, Wordsworth met the poet Samuel Taylor Coleridge. Together, the two poets published *Lyrical Ballads,* introducing Romanticism to England. Wordsworth's poems used the language of every day speech, and celebrated ordinary things. They also reflected Wordsworth's relationship with nature. Wordsworth, who spent most of his life in the natural splendor of the Lake District, depicts the relationship of man with nature as the relationship between the mind and the world, or the soul with God. The central place of nature and of the self in his poetry created a new poetic tradition. Wordsworth was one of England's greatest poets.

Wright, Frank Lloyd (1867-1959)American architect. Born in Wisconsin, Wright grew up on a farm. After studying engineering, he worked for Chicago architect Louis H. Sullivan whose philosophy of "form follows function" profoundly influenced Wright. In 1893, Wright began building houses in his "prairie style" – long, low houses that hugged the earth. Wright's buildings relate harmoniously to their natural surroundings. He omits many interior walls to create open, flowing interior spaces. One of Wright's most famous designs is Fallingwater, built in 1936. Cantilevered dramatically over a waterfall, surrounded by trees visible from every room, Fallingwater exemplifies the intimate relationship between house and surroundings that Wright advocated. Wright's sensitivity to a building's environment, his creative use of materials, particularly concrete and cement blocks, and his beautiful and original designs helped revolutionize 20th century architecture.

Yeats, William Butler (1865-1939). Irish writer. Yeats grew up in London, spending vacations in County Sligo, Ireland, which became the setting of many of his poems. In 1881 he returned to Dublin, his birthplace, where he studied painting. His father was a Pre-Raphaelite painter. Yeats' love of Ireland and his interest in mysticism were central elements of his life and work. In his early poems and plays, he uses mystical lyrical verse to examine the themes of Irish mythology and Irish nationalism. His later poems are sparer, and more intellectual, although the spiritual continues to be an important theme. Yeats led a literary renaissance in Ireland. He served in the Irish Senate from 1922 to 1928. A major figure in 20th century literature, Yeats won the Nobel Prize in 1923.

Yogananda, Paramahansa (1893-1952). Indian mystic. Born in Gorakhpur, India, Yogananda became a monk after graduating from Calcutta University in 1914. He founded a school in Calcutta, and in 1920 moved to the Unites States, where he traveled the country lecturing and teaching *kriya yoga,* a type of meditation.

Notes